THE
MYSTIC
GRAIL

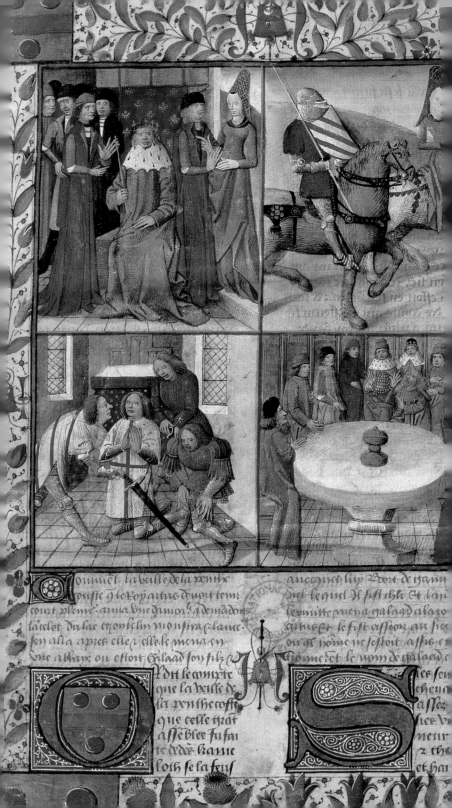

ouuint la beille dela penthe
couste q̃ le roy artus deuott tenir
court plemer aruia vne damon q̃ demadoit
laūcelot dulac etonsilm monstra plante.
son alla apres elle/ellele mena en
vne abbaye ou estoit Galaad son filz q̃

Dit le counte
que les beille de
la penthecoste
q̃ celle trat
assee susan
te dedes ame
loth se la frist

aucaynes luy Bort de ihann
nel lequel il fist chle Et lan
lermitte mena galaad alaro
atruge se fist asseoir au sieg
on q̃ hoine ne sestoit asses e
homedet le nom de galaad e

les sei
cheur
assez
les vi
menir
z the
et hai

THE MYSTIC GRAIL

*The Challenge of
the Arthurian Quest*

JOHN MATTHEWS

Sterling Publishing Co., Inc.
New York

for Barbara Finn
Companion on the Quest

Library of Congress
Cataloging-in-Publication Data Available

1 2 3 4 5 6 7 8 9 10

Published in 1997 by Sterling Publishing Company, Inc.
387 Park Avenue South, New York, N.Y. 10016

Originally published in Great Britain in 1997 by Godsfield Press

© 1997 by Godsfield Press

Text © 1997 by John Matthews

Designed and produced by The Bridgewater Book Company

Picture Research by Lynda Marshall

Distributed in Canada by Sterling Publishing
c/o Canadian Manda Group, One Atlantic Avenue, Suite 105
Toronto, Ontario, Canada M6K 3E7

Printed and bound in Hong Kong

Sterling ISBN 0-8069-9604-8

The publishers wish to thank the following for the use of pictures:

Birmingham Museums & Art Gallery: pp. 40–41

Bodleian Library, Oxford: pp. 18 MS Rawl QB6.f.246; 23 MS Rawl QB6.f.246; 60 MS Douce
214.f.14; 62 MS Rawl Q66.f.174; 66 MS Rawl Q66.f.155; 73 MS Douce 178.f.309; 78–79
MS Douce 215.f.39V.

Bridgeman Art Library, London: Cover, pp. 2 Musée Conde, Chantilly; 6 Palazzo Ducale,
Urbino; 13 National Gallery, London; 24–25 Phillips Fine Art Auctioneers; 29 Lady Lever
Gallery, Port Sunlight; 31 Victoria & Albert Museum; 34 Bibliothèque Nationale; 44 Walker
Art Gallery, Liverpool; 48–49 Southampton City Art Gallery; 54 Bibliothèque Nationale; 57
Fine Art Society, London; 58 Bibliothèque Nationale; 68–69 Bibliothèque Nationale; 80–81
Birmingham Museums & Art Gallery; 82–83 Birmingham Museums & Art Gallery.

e.t.archive, London: pp. 9, 16, 19, 39, 43, 51.

Fine Art Photographs London: pp. 71, 74.

Tate Gallery, London: pp. 86–87.

Cover: Emblem of Passion, French, late 15th century
Frontispiece: Roman de Tristran; King Arthur; Lancelot and the Lady;
the arming of Sir Galahad, late 15th century

CONTENTS

INTRODUCTION

The story of the Grail is one of the crowning glories of the Western imagination. No one can say precisely where or when it emerged. Indeed, it seems to have always been present, hidden in the deepest recesses of the human soul. Certainly, it has continued to exert a powerful fascination over all who come in contact with it. This is not surprising, since it deals with themes that are as important today as they have always been — the search for absolutes, the quest for healing, and the. unending quest for truth.

The Grail has been described as many things: as a stone, fallen from the crown of the Angel of Light during the war in Heaven; as a Cauldron of Celtic antiquity sought after by heroes; as the cup used by Christ to celebrate the Last Supper and the first Eucharist. But, more than the sum of its parts, the Grail is really an idea that represents the presence

of a numinous, mystical link between the sacred and the secular. It remains, to this very day, a focus for those who seek and a provider of wonder amid the colorless outer world in which we live.

In as much as we can say anything about the beginnings of the long history of the Grail, we must look first of all to the stories that circulated among the Celtic peoples. There, we find references to an ancient, magical vessel known as the Cauldron. One such object is described in a poem attributed to the 6th-century bard Taliesin. It was not written down in its present form until the 9th century, but the story it tells predates this by several hundred years. Much is already in place however – the idea of a quest, undertaken by no lesser person than Arthur (still a warrior rather than a king) and his followers. They sail in a magical ship, through stormy waters to Annwn – one of the names for the Otherworld – in search of a magical vessel guarded by nine priestesses. There are seven towers, or

"caers," in this place, in each of which is a different challenge to be overcome. The outcome of the voyage is uncertain, for only seven of the original "three shiploads" return, and we are not told if they brought the Cauldron with them.

Since my song resounded
in the turning Caer,
I am pre-eminent. My first song
Was of the Cauldron itself.
Nine maidens kindled
it with their breath
Of what nature was it?
Pearls were about its rim,
Nor would it boil a coward's portion.
Lleminawg thrust his flashing sword
Deep within it;
And before dark gates, a light was lifted.
When we went with Arthur –
a mighty labor
Save seven, none returned
from Caer Fedwydd.

Pre-eminent am I
Since my song resounded
In the four-square city,
The Island of the Strong Door.
The light was dim and mixed
with darkness,
Though bright wine was set before us.
Three shiploads of Prydwen went
with Arthur –
Save seven, none returned
from Caer Rigor....

TALIESIN TRANS. J.MATTHEWS

Prieddeu Annwn

LEFT: ONE SCHOOL OF THOUGHT NAMES THE GRAIL AS THE CUP USED BY CHRIST AT THE LAST SUPPER, HERE DEPICTED BY JUSTE DE GAND (FL. 1660–75).

This is probably the oldest reference we have to a quest, undertaken by Arthur and his men, for a mysterious vessel. After this we hear nothing more of the story until the beginning of the 12th century, when the French court poet Chrétien de Troyes composed a poem called *Perceval, or The Story of the Grail*. It told the story of a search undertaken by a simple youth, brought up away from the ways of men, for a mysterious object known as the "Graal." But Chrétien left the poem unfinished, and in so doing he created a mystery that managed to stir the imagination of seekers ever since.

Over the next hundred years the story was told and retold, each author adding his or her own touches, deepening and building upon hints offered by Chrétien's poem. The Grail itself went through a number of transformations — a factor that became part of its nature — so it could not be codified or pinned down to a single image or idea. In the versions that followed, the Grail was variously described as a cup, a dish, a stone, or a jewel. It acquired a family of guardians, one of whom, the Wounded King, ruled over a devastated Waste Land. This theme, the wounding of the king and the quest for healing, became a central part of the story, and out of it arose the idea of the search for the castle where the miraculous vessel was kept — initially by the knights of the Round Table, but in subsequent ages, our own included, by anyone who has the courage to seek out the miraculous vessel. At first only a select few could find their way to the elusive castle, and once there they had to pose a question — Whom does the Grail serve? — which, in some mysterious fashion, could bring about healing to the Wounded King, to the land over which he ruled and, by inference, to the seeker also. In our own time the Quest has itself become the

objective of all people, and the healing of Waste Land and Wounded King can be seen as metaphors for our own inner dry places and the wounds we have suffered in our journey through life.

When King Arthur and his knights held court at Camelot to celebrate the feast of Pentecost, they first beheld the Grail in all its wonder and mystery in their midst. In the words of Sir Thomas Malory, whose 15th-century version of the legend vividly captures the story:

There entered into the hall the Holy Grail, covered with white samite, that there was none might see it, nor who bear it. And then was the hall filled with good odors, and every knight had such meats and drinks as he loved best of this world.

SIR THOMAS MALORY

Le Morte d'Arthur

(BOOK XIII, CH.9.)

THE GOOD SIR GALAHAD, AS DEPICTED BY DANTE GABRIEL ROSSETTI (ABOVE LEFT), WAS ONE OF THE KNIGHTS OF THE ROUND TABLE WHO, TOGETHER WITH ARTHUR, BEHELD THE GRAIL AT THE FEAST OF PENTECOST (ABOVE).

The gift of the Grail is just this: it gives us the ability to see clearly. In addition it offers spiritual nourishment, the food of the soul.

Astonished and moved by their experience, everyone of the Round Table fellowship pledged to seek this wonder and not to rest until they had found out more about it. Their Quest was to change them, utterly. Many would never return but became lost in the wild forests or "the Lands Adventurous." Those who did succeed faced countless trials and tests that proved more than their physical courage. Thus, when the pure and sinless knight Galahad, one of the very few who could claim any degree of success in the great endeavor, reached the Grail Castle and entered into its mystery, he received a vision in which he heard himself and his followers addressed as those "who in the midst of this life have become spiritual creatures" (*Le Morte d'Arthur*). This, surely, is one of the secrets at the heart of the Grail — that to look upon it, even to seek it, is to discover a spiritual dimension that lies at the heart of our own lives.

We too can be transformed into spiritual creatures, and the daily miracle of the Grail procession, in which the vessel is borne before us as it was before the knights in the story, demands that we dare to ask ourselves the Grail question. That question — Whom does the Grail serve? — brings an answer that all who follow the path to the Grail must sooner or later know — that it serves each and every one of us, according to our needs and according to the degree of service that we ourselves can offer. This is, indeed, more than caring for others; rather, it is maintaining a kind of spiritual partnership with the rest of the universe. When we work with the spiritual aspect of our nature, we discover new levels of service and find therein a very real sense of exchange that is perhaps the most profound aspect of the message of the Grail.

The Grail can be many things; indeed, it can manifest in almost any number of ways. It may have more than one form, or no form at all; it may not even exist in this dimension. Yet it provides us with an object of personal search, a quest from which may come personal growth and the restoration of the spirit. It is for all who seek this High Mystery of the Grail (so called by more than one of its authors) that this book is intended.

It cannot tell the whole story, for that is still being written. But it does contain some bright glimpses into the magical world of the Arthurian Grail Quest, described in quotations taken primarily from medieval sources, since it is these authors who gave us the story as we still know it today.

Indeed, despite the fact that we have come a long way since the 12th century, there is still much that we recognize in these works from our own spiritual Quest. All the works quoted here have one thing in common – they reflect the numinous quality of the Grail, its mystic truth, and the extraordinary effect it has had on ordinary seekers throughout time. It was this effect that the unknown author of the mysterious 12th-century text known simply as *The Elucidation* described so eloquently:

In very truth it was [because of] this finding of the ... Grail ...
that the waters which ran not, and the fountains which flowed not...
ran forth amidst the meadows.
Then were the fields green and bountiful, and the woods clad in leaves, the day that the Court [of the Grail] was found.
Throughout the country were the forests so great and thick, so fair and fresh, that every wayfarer journeying through the land did marvel thereat.

The Elucidation

We can still, if we so desire, make our own journey to that land. And we too will only be able to marvel at the green and verdant place within ourselves, wherein lies an even greater mystery, waiting for us to discover it. Meditation on the themes and images surrounding the Grail can enable its visionary presence to flow into our daily lives. If worked with in this way, the story can bring real healing, even enlightenment, to our burdened lives. The vision of the Grail is one that may seem at times almost more than we can bear; yet its voice offers both comfort and illumination in the midst of the greatest darkness.

JOHN MATTHEWS, OXFORD, 1996

C h a p t e r   O n e

THE COMING
OF THE GRAIL

The early history of the Grail is a catalog of wonders and miracles. Here the realm of the spirit breaks through continually into the realm of the everyday. The presence of the Grail acts as a catalyst, establishing a center of power and enlightenment on earth. In time it becomes the object of a profound search – the Quest – which will test those who set out upon it to the utmost limits of their humanity and beyond into the place where the hidden treasures of the spirit lie waiting for those with the courage and vision to discover them. The Grail itself is one such treasure, and those who stand in its presence are changed from that moment onward.

Forever linked with the early history of the Grail is Joseph of Arimathea, who in Christian apocryphal literature is called the "uncle" of Jesus. He it was who, after the events of the Crucifixion, requested the body of Christ from Pontius Pilate and placed it in a tomb meant for himself. After the disappearance of the body, Joseph was thrown into prison and left to die. He survived the ordeal, sustained by the power of the Grail, which was given into his hands by the risen Christ.

Released, years later, Joseph gathers a small band of disciples and sets forth on a journey that will bring him, in time, to the shores of Britain. The Grail goes with them, and many wonders and miraculous events take place as they travel across Europe, sometimes staying in one place, at other times moving on – always in search of a place to house the Grail, a home where others could come to revere it. On one occasion things are going ill with the little company, and Joseph kneels before the Grail to seek understanding of their problems. He receives it, and in the process more of the history of the Grail is revealed.

ABOVE: JOSEPH OF ARIMATHEA RECEIVES THE BODY OF
CHRIST AT THE ENTOMBMENT BY MICHELANGELO
(1475–1564). JOSEPH WAS LATER TO RECEIVE THE GRAIL
FROM THE RISEN CHRIST AND THEN TO JOURNEY ACROSS
EUROPE SEARCHING FOR A HOME FOR THE CUP.

Joseph went to the Grail and knelt before it weeping, and he said, "Oh Lord, you wanted to consort with us because of your love for us and to save your creatures, who wished to obey you and follow your will. I saw you dead, as truly I saw you living, and after death I saw you alive and speaking to me in the tower in which I was held. There, Lord, you commanded me, when you brought me this Grail, that whenever I wanted to know your secrets, I should come before this precious Grail, which contains your glorious blood. Therefore, I ask you to advise me on the matter, for my people are starving."

ABOVE: AN ENGRAVING BY WILLIAM BLAKE (1757–1827) SHOWS JOSEPH OF ARIMATHEA ARRIVING ON THE SHORES OF BRITAIN IN HIS QUEST FOR A RESTING PLACE FOR THE GRAIL.

Then the voice of the Holy Spirit spoke to Joseph: "Joseph, do not be dismayed; you are not to blame in this matter."

"Then, Sir, let me remove those who have sinned from my company."

"You cannot do that, Joseph; but I command you to take the Grail of my blood and to test those sinners with it. Remember that I was sold and betrayed by someone who ate with me. The person who did this thing was ashamed and left, and was never again my disciple. No one shall take his place until you are sitting there. Summon Bron, your brother-in-law, who is a good man. Get him to go down to the water to catch fish and bring the first one he catches to you. Place it on that table, with the Grail, and cover it with a napkin. Then call together all your people and tell them that they shall see why they have been so afflicted. And when you have taken your seat where I sat at the Last Supper, seat Bron on your right and you will see that Bron will not take that place. The empty place signifies the seat of Judas, who left when he saw that he had betrayed me. That place may not be filled until Enygeus has her husband Bron's child, and when the child is born he shall be assigned that place. When you have done all this, call your people and tell them, if they *believe in God the Father of all the world, and in the Son and Holy Ghost, and in all the commandments and teachings I gave them when I spoke to them through you of the three virtues that are one, if they have upheld all these well, let them come and take their seats by the grace of Our Lord."* [1]

A wondrous thing, hidden in the flower garden of the king where the elect of all nations are called.

WOLFRAM VON ESCHENBACH:

Parzival

From the miracle of the fish that feeds the company so miraculously, their leader becomes known by a new title, "The Rich Fisherman." In time this was to be changed to "The Fisher King," a title that resonates with the mystery of the one who bears it, who is guardian of the wondrous Grail.

Some time after the events narrated above, we learn of a certain holy man named Titurel who is called upon to build a great temple to house the Grail. This takes place long before the days of Arthur and tells us something of the Grail's history before the knights of the Round Table set forth on their great Quest. Titurel himself is one of a family of guardians who were appointed by Joseph of Arimathea and his descendants to keep the Grail for a future time.

When Titurel was 50 years old, an angel appeared to him and said that the rest of his life should be devoted to the service of the Grail. The angel led him into a wilderness, Foreis Salvasch, which was overgrown with many exotic plants and trees. Strange birds filled the air with song, and hidden in the earth were countless precious stones. In the center of the forest was Mount Salvasch, which had always been concealed and protected from fallen humanity, whether Christian, Jew, or heathen. The mountain and everything on it was protected from all evil. Titurel found encamped there workers from all the nations of the earth to assist him in his work. The Grail could be seen hovering over the mountain, held by the invisible hands of angels. Titurel built a great castle on the mountain, from where he did battle against the heathen, until no one dare enter the land of Salvaterre.

Titurel resolved to build a temple for the Grail, using only the purest of materials. He asked advice from those

❖

ABOVE: THE GRAIL WAS KEPT SAFE WITHIN THE
WALLS OF THE GRAIL CASTLE THROUGH THE DARK
DAYS, WAITING FOR THE QUEST OF THE KNIGHTS
OF THE ROUND TABLE.

learned in the properties of precious stones, as once taught by Pythagoras and Hercules. They told him of the fire-stone abestus, which sends forth a fire that does not burn; and the water-stone elitropia, whose water is cool in the summer and warm in the winter. These were chosen as the basic materials of the temple. Everywhere precious stones and metals were used; only the chairs, lest they should be cold, were make of wood.

Titurel cleared away part of the summit, which consisted of a single piece of onyx, and polished its surface until it glowed like the moon. One morning he found engraved in the stone the ground plan for the temple. Recognizing the Grail as the source of inspiration, he arranged for construction to begin.

The work took 30 years to complete. During this time the Grail supplied the workers with all their needs; it sent forth the precious substances from which the temple was built, as well as food and drink. These gifts more than outweighed those given by God to Solomon for the temple in Jerusalem. [2] ✠

In the land of Salvation, in the Forest of Salvation, lies a solitary mountain called Muntsalvach, which King Titurel surrounded by a wall and on which he built a costly castle to serve as the Temple of the Grail;

because the Grail in that time had no fixed place, but floated, invisible, in the air.

ALBRECHT VON SCHARFENBURG

Der Jungere Titurel

Thus the Grail remained for many years enshrined in this wondrous palace, built with the aid of angels. The family of the Grail kept it safe, harboring it against the dark days that were to come and the beginning of the great Quest. Thus we come to a time near the beginning of Arthur's reign, and to a moment of profound significance, a prelude to the wonders and terrors that were to shake the kingdom of Logres to its foundations.

Among the first knights to join Arthur was a wild and willful figure, Balin le Sauvage. He was widely known for his hot temper and was often imprisoned for his acts. But it so happened that he was at liberty when a damsel arrived at the court asking for help, and so began Balin's adventure. Falling in with another knight, he saw this man killed by an unseen assailant, and learned that an evil prince named Garlon was responsible.

Pursuing Garlon, Balin found himself in a castle where he was made welcome, but the castle concealed a great secret. What followed was to change forever the course of events in Arthur's realm.

✠ Then Balin was brought unto a chamber and unarmed; and they would have had Balin leave his sword behind him. "Nay," said Balin, "that do I not, for it is the custom of my country for a knight always to keep his weapon with him." Then they gave him leave to wear his sword, and so he went unto the castle, and was set among knights of worship.

Soon Balin asked, "Is there not a knight in this court whose name is Garlon?" "Yonder he goeth," said a knight, "he with the black face; he is the marvellest knight now living, for he goeth invisible." "Ah well," said Balin, "is that he?" Then Balin thought him long: If I slay him here I shall not escape, and if I leave him now, I may never meet with him again and much harm he will do, if he lives. Therewith Garlon espied that Balin beheld him, and he came and smote Balin on the face with the back of his hand, and said, "Knight, why beholdest me so? For shame therefore, eat thy meat and do what thou came for." "This is not the first despite that thou hast done me," said Balin, "therefore I will do what I came for," and he rose up fiercely and clave Garlon's head to the shoulders.

Anon all the knights arose from the table for to set on Balin, and King Pellam himself arose up fiercely, and said, "Knight, hast thou slain my brother? Thou shalt die therefor." "Well," said Balin, "do it yourself." "Yes," said King Pellam, "no man shall have ado with thee but myself." Then King Pellam caught in his hand a grim weapon and smote eagerly at Balin; but Balin put the sword betwixt his head and the stroke, and therewith his sword broke. And when Balin was weaponless he ran into a chamber to seek some weapon, and so from chamber to chamber, and no weapon he could find, and always King

BALIN'S GREAT ADVENTURE ENDED WHEN HE STRUCK THE DOLOROUS BLOW AGAINST KING PELLAM (ABOVE) WITH A SPEAR THAT HE FOUND IN A CHAMBER, RICHLY ARRAYED WITH GOLD AND SILVER (ABOVE RIGHT).

*Pellam after him. And at the last he
entered into a chamber that was
marvellously well arrayed and richly,
and a bed with cloth of gold. And
thereby stood a table of gold with four
pillars of silver that bare up the table,
and upon the table stood a marvellous
spear strangely wrought. And when Balin
saw that spear, he got it in his hand and
turned him to King Pellam, and smote
him passingly sore with that spear, that
King Pellam fell down in a swoon, and
therewith the castle roof and walls brake
and fell to the earth, and Balin fell
down so that he might not stir foot nor*

*hand. And so the most part of the castle
was fallen down through that dolorous
stroke, and lay upon Pellam and Balin
three days.* [3] ✠

Neither Balin nor Pellam is killed
by this destructive act. Balin lives
to follow the path of adventure farther — though his death comes soon
after. Pellam, however, suffers a
more terrible fate. The wound that
he received from the spear, which
was a holy relic believed to be that
used by the Centurion Longinus
to pierce the side of Christ, will

not heal. Only the coming of a promised savior can bring this about, and the secondary objective of the Grail Quest will be a search for that healing. The effects are not limited to the Wounded King – the land over which he rules becomes wasted, desolate, and dead. The mystical link between king and country is such that when one is wounded, the other suffers also. In time it becomes a metaphor for all human woundedness, and the Quest for the Grail a search for the healing of that state.

That was only the first of a succession of events that pointed the way toward the coming of the Grail and the beginning of the great Quest that was to take so many of the fellowship of the Round Table into the realm of the spirit, where they would encounter many terrible tests and trials. In many of the stories, Arthur himself maintains a passive role in these events, never setting forth from the court but awaiting news of his knights. In this extract, however, he goes forth alone and receives a rare and wonderful vision of the mysteries of the Grail.

ABOVE: ARTHUR RECEIVES A STRANGE MANTLE: A SCENE FROM THOMAS MALORY'S LE MORTE D'ARTHUR, ILLUSTRATED BY AUBREY BEARDSLEY (1872–98).

King Arthur rode into the forest and came upon the chapel of St. Augustine, where a hermit was about to sing the mass. The king tied his horse to a tree and decided to enter the chapel. But, to his mortification, he was unable to enter, although there was no one there to stop him and the door was open. The king looked at the hermit and saw at his right hand the fairest child he had ever seen; he was dressed in a white robe and wore a golden crown leaded with precious stones that shone in the light. On the hermit's left side was a lady so fair that her beauty was beyond compare. When the holy hermit had said his confession and approached the altar, the lady took her son and went to sit on a jeweled chair to the right of the altar. She placed her son upon her knees and, kissing him sweetly, said, "Sir, you are my father and my son and my lord, and guardian of me and of all the world." King Arthur marveled that she should call the child her father and her son. At the moment the mass was begun, the king saw a light come through the window and shine upon the altar; it was brighter than any ray from the sun, moon, or stars. The king was angered that he could not enter the chapel to hear the hermit sing the mass and the beautiful responses that seemed like the singing of angels. When the holy gospel was read, the lady took her child and offered him into the hands of the hermit. The hermit set the child upon the altar and began the sacrament. King Arthur went down on his knees and began to pray. As he looked toward the altar, it seemed that the hermit held between his hands a man who was bleeding from his side and in his palms and feet, and was crowned with thorns. As he looked at the man, the king had pity in his heart and tears in his eyes. He looked again at the altar and saw that the figure of the man had changed into the child he had seen before.

When the mass was sung, the voice of a holy angel sang Ite, missa est. The son took the mother by the hand and vanished from the chapel; the flame that came though the window went away with them. [4] ✠

The association of the Grail with the central mysteries of Christianity continued to deepen throughout the Middle Ages. Galahad, the sinless knight who will come closest to the heart of the mystery, is often identified with Christ, and the miraculous transubstantiation of wine into blood becomes a central part of the Grail's visionary impulse.

Even as Arthur received the vision of the Virgin, in another part of the kingdom one of his greatest knights — some said the best knight in all the world — was embarking on an adventure that would bring him in close contact with the mystery and introduce a new hero, one who would go farther than any other in the pursuit of holiness and the spiritual path.

Lancelot — for it is of him that we speak — had many adventures, but none more strange than that in which he rescued a lady from a bath of boiling water and slew a dragon in her honor. But the outcome of this adventure was to be very different from anything he

might have imagined, for all of these events took place in the realm of the Grail, and the lady was the Princess of the Grail.

✠ Therwithal came King Pelles, the good and noble knight, and saluted Sir Launcelot. "Fair knight," said the king, "what is your name?"

"Sir," said Launcelot, "my name is Sir Launcelot du Lake." "And my name is," said the king, "Pelles, king of the foreign country, and cousin nigh unto Joseph of Armathie." And then either of them made much of other, and went into the castle to take their repast. And anon there came in a dove at a window, and in her mouth there seemed a little censer of gold. And there was such a savour as all the spicery of the world had been there.

And forthwith there was upon the table all manner of meats and drinks. So came in a damosel passing fair and young, and she bare a vessel of gold betwixt her hands. "O Jesu," said Sir Launcelot, "what may this mean?" "This is," said the king, "the richest thing that any man hath living. And when this thing goeth about, the Round Table shall be broken; and wit thou well," said the king, "this is the holy Sangreal that ye have here seen."

And fain would King Pelles have found the means to have had Sir Launcelot lay by his daughter, fair Elaine. For this intent: the king knew well that Sir Launcelot should get a child upon his daughter, the which should be named Sir Galahad the good knight, by whom all the foreign country should be brought out of danger, and by him the Holy Greal should be achieved.

Then came forth a lady named Dame

Brisen, and she said unto the king: "Sir, wit ye well Sir Launcelot loveth no lady in the wold but Queen Guenever; therefore I shall make him to lie with your daughter, and he shall believe that he lieth with Queen Guenever." "O fair lady, Dame Brisen," said the king, "hope ye to bring this about?" "Sir," said she, "upon pain of my life let me deal"; for this Brisen was one of the greatest enchantresses that was at that time in the world living. Then anon she made one come to Sir Launcelot that he knew well. And this man brought him a ring from Queen Guenever like as it had come from her, and such one as she was wont to wear; and when Sir Launcelot saw that token wit ye well he was never so glad. "Where is my lady?" said Sir Launcelot. "In the Castle of Case," said the messenger, "but five mile hence." Then Sir Launcelot thought to be there the

---

✠

THE DASHING AND ROMANTIC SIR LANCELOT WAS DOOMED TO FAILURE IN HIS QUEST BECAUSE OF HIS PASSIONATE BUT ILLICIT LOVE FOR GUINEVERE (LEFT). BUT OUT OF THIS LOVE CAME GALAHAD, SON OF LANCELOT AND ELAINE, DAUGHTER OF KING PELLES. LANCELOT WAS TRICKED INTO LYING WITH ELAINE WHOM HE BELIEVED TO BE GUINEVERE (BELOW).

OVERLEAF: LANCELOT AND GUINEVERE BY HERBERT JAMES DRAPER (1864–1920).

same night. And then Brisen by the commandment of King Pelles let send Elaine with twenty-five knights unto the Castle of Case. Sir Launcelot against night rode unto that castle, and there anon he was received worshipfully with such people, to his seeming, as were about Queen Guenever secret.

When Sir Launcelot was alighted, he asked where the queen was. Dame Brisen said she was in her bed; and then the people were avoided, and Sir Launcelot was led unto his chamber. And Dame Brisen brought Sir Launcelot a cup full of wine; and anon as he had drunken that wine he was so assotted and mad *that he might make no delay, but withouten any let he went to bed; and he weened that the maiden Elaine had been Queen Guenever. Wit you well that Sir Launcelot was glad, and so was that lady Elaine that she had gotten Sir Launcelot in her arms. For well she knew that same night should be gotten upon her Galahad that should prove the best knight of the world; and so they lay together until the morn; and all the windows and holes of that chamber were stopped that no manner of day might be seen.* ✠

Here we see the wounded King Pelles reaching out for healing. Tired of waiting for the arrival of the knight who will bring an end to his suffering and renewal to the wasted lands over which he rules, he takes steps to engender a hero who will achieve the Grail for all. Thus, in the human dimension of the Quest, those who suffer their own wounds of the spirit seek healing by turning outward, by asking the question: "Whom does the Grail serve?" The answer to this, which is variously given as "the king" and "yourself," is in reality less important than the act of asking it. Nevertheless, it triggers the healing impulse for both the Wounded King and the Waste Land, while for the quester it sets in motion a movement toward self-fulfillment.

From this action on the part of Lancelot comes the child who will grow up to become the greatest of all the Grail seekers – Galahad. And thus by a marvelous stroke of fate or the workings of the greater mystery, of which the Grail is but a part – out of the forbidden love of Lancelot for Arthur's queen, – comes the redeeming figure of the perfect Grail knight. Here, as throughout so much of the long tale of the Quest, we see how all is planned and ordained in a miraculous fashion, so that the achieving of the Grail is foreseen even before it makes its first appearance to Arthur and his knights. For those of us who set forth in search of truths in our own time, there are many metaphors here that will strike a chord within. Our own journey may be fraught with trials and tests not unlike those endured by the Quest knights. For us as for them, the Grail remains an object of vision and inner search that will lead to our transformation.

✠

ABOVE LEFT: AUBREY BEARDSLEY'S ILLUSTRATION (1893) OF ONLOOKERS AT THE BEGUILING OF LANCELOT BY ELAINE.

C h a p t e r   T w o

THE QUEST BEGINS

The coming of the Grail is foreshadowed by signs and wonders. A strange enchantment lies over the land of Logres, King Arthur's magical realm, where knights do battle with evil in many forms and offer help to all who are in need. The first appearances of the Grail are as mysterious as they are miraculous, and it is not hard to understand the inspiration felt by the Arthurian knights when they first caught sight of the marvelous vessel, of which they had already heard many wonders. Merlin himself had prophesied its coming and the trials and adventures that would befall those who took up the Quest. It was known that many who set forth from Camelot would not return. But, despite this, the knights were eager to set forth.

Their Quest was for neither glory nor earthly reward, but opened a gateway into the spiritual realm, where the trials and tests were those of spirit over flesh, of honor over strength, and where the inner truth of the Grail could be made itself profoundly manifest.

It took a rare kind of person to set out upon the Quest, and few were to succeed wholly in their aims. Yet heroes there were, as well as heroines, whose sole reason for existing was the achievement of the Grail. Three names ring loudly in the role of honor: Perceval, Galahad, and Bors. Others, such as Lancelot and

---

ABOVE: MERLIN, ILLUSTRATED BY AUBREY BEARDSLEY. RIGHT: THE BEGUILING OF MERLIN BY SIR EDWARD BURNE-JONES (1833-98). MERLIN THE MAGICIAN AND KING ARTHUR'S MENTOR PROPHESIED THE COMING OF THE GRAIL AND TOLD OF THE THREE KNIGHTS WHO WOULD ULTIMATELY BE SUCCESSFUL IN THEIR QUEST.

sit in the Perilous Seat, which in the allegory of the Grail search represented the place occupied by Christ at the table of the Last Supper. Only one who was pure in heart and single-minded in the desire to achieve the mystery of the Grail could sit in this seat. In our own time, the search may well lead us to sit at another kind of Round Table, that of our own soul, where only a true dedication to the Quest will permit us to see the potential within ourselves.

Gawain, fail, but in so glorious a manner that their stories must be told as well. And there is another – Dindraine, Perceval's sister – who saw a vision of the Grail long before any of them. She gave up her life for another, thereby coming to the spiritual heart of the Grail in a marvellous way.

But before any of these had appeared, Merlin had prophesied the coming of the Grail or, as it was known then, the Sangreal or "Holy" Grail, and proclaimed that nothing would ever be the same again. He spoke also of the three great knights, whom he called "three white bulls." Only one of these knights, Galahad, would be fit to

When Merlin had ordained the Round Table he said, by them which should be fellows of the Round Table the truth of the Holy Grail should be well known. And men asked him how men might know them that should do best to enchieve the Holy Grail? Then he said there should be three white bulls that should enchieve it, and the two should be maidens, and the third should be chaste. And that one of the three should pass his father as much as the lion passeth the

---

MERLIN AND NIMUE BY AUBREY BEARDSLEY (LEFT) AND BY SIR EDWARD BURNE-JONES (RIGHT). NIMUE USED HER CHARMS TO ENTICE MERLIN INTO REVEALING HIS MAGIC TO HER AND THEN USED IT TO ENCHANT MERLIN AND IMPRISON HIM IN A CAVE.

leopard, both of strength and hardiness.

They that heard Merlin say so said thus: "Since there shall be such a knight, thou shouldest ordain by thy crafts a seat, that no man should sit in it but he all only that shall pass all other knights." Then Merlin answered that he would do so. And then he made the Siege Perilous, in the which Galahad sat... [1]

All of this took place before the great events of the Quest. Yet already the marvellous constellation of heroes was beginning to be drawn toward the Arthurian court, where, soon, the Grail would appear. Perceval of Wales, the first of the Quest knights to experience the mysteries of the castle in which the mystic vessel was housed, grew up in the depths of the forest; he had been taken there while still a baby by his mother, who desired that he should know nothing of the ways of men.

Perceval knowing little of the world, would come to be known as "the Perfect Fool" because of his innocence. And yet he was the first to undertake the Quest. The story of his coming is a pattern of laughter and the marvellous.

It was the spring, when all things are aflame with joy, when the son of the widow lady of the lonely wild forest arose and saddled his hunter, took three javelins, and left his mother's manor. He entered the forest and at once rejoiced at the sweet season and the sounds of the birds. The lad began to cast his javelins until he heard five armed knights approaching. Their armor made a great crashing noise as they came through the forest. The noble youth, who heard but did not see the knights, thought, "By my soul, my mother told me the truth when she said that devils are the most terrible thing in the world and taught me that one ought to cross oneself against them. But I scorn her teaching and will not cross myself; rather I will strike the strongest with one of the javelins I am carrying, so that none of the others, I think, will dare to come near me."

But when the youth saw the knights clearly, with their jingling coats of mail, their bright, gleaming helmets, their lances and shields, and their bright colors catching the light of the sun, he was so delighted that he exclaimed, "Lord God, have mercy! These are angels that I see. Alas, I was very wrong when I said they were devils. My mother, who told me that angels are more beautiful than anything else, was telling me no lie. Here I see God himself, I think, for one of them is so fair that the others have not a tenth

of his beauty. My mother herself said that one must believe in God and adore and bow the knee and honor Him. I will adore this one and the others too."

He threw himself on the ground, reciting the prayers his mother had taught him. The master of the knights saw him and said, "Stay back, for this youth has fallen on the ground in fear at the sight of us. If we all went together toward him, he may be so frightened that he would die and could not answer any of our questions."

The knights stopped, and their leader went quickly to the youth, greeted and reassured him, saying, "Young sir, do not be afraid."

"I am not afraid," said the youth, "by the Savior in whom I believe. Are you God?"

"No, by my faith."

"Who are you then?"

"I am a knight."

"I have not known a knight," said the youth, "nor have I seen one, nor ever heard talk of one. But you are more beautiful than God. If only I could be like you, so shining and shaped just so!" [2]

The marvellous Perceval has not yet learned not to ask questions, and his mistaking of Arthur's knights for "angels" expresses the boyish curiosity that is to lead him, ultimately, to the beginning of his great adventure.

As so often in the search for truth, Perceval's quest was to be a story of steps forward and backward, of turns and twists. Setting

RIGHT: NACIEN THE HERMIT, WHO SENT GALAHAD TO KING ARTHUR. NACIEN WAS BLINDED WHEN HE CAME TOO CLOSE TO THE GRAIL BUT WAS CURED WITH DROPS OF BLOOD FROM THE BLEEDING LANCE.

✠

ABOVE: BEFORE LEAVING ON HIS QUEST FOR THE GRAIL,
GALAHAD RECEIVED HIS SWORD AND SPURS IN THE
RITUAL OF KNIGHTHOOD, SEEN HERE IN THE
MANUSCRIPT OF TRISTAN (1463).

town. When the minstrels saw the knight in the cart they followed, shouting and pelting mud and old rags at him.[4] ✠

Somewhere between the perfection of Galahad and the worldliness of Lancelot and Gawain stands the figure of Bors. Lancelot's cousin, and one of the great knights of the Round Table, he is invariably represented as the most human of the successful questers. He is, to all intents and purposes, an everyman figure, who struggles with all his might to attain the supreme heights of spiritual chivalry to which Galahad and Perceval seem so well fitted. As such, he is perhaps the most humanly recognizable of all the Grail heroes – human in his weakness and inability to see beyond the moment in which he is living. Like many who embark upon the Quest today, he is often faced, as in this next passage, with excruciating choices.

Before Oedipus was
the Maymed King is.
In his castle the lance bleeds, the horn
bleeds, the tusk bleeds.

JOHN MORIARTY

Turtle Was Gone A Long Time

✠ *Upon the morn, as soon as the day appeared, Bors departed and so rode into a forest unto the hour of midday, and there befell him a marvellous adventure. He met at the departing of two ways two knights that led Lionel, his brother, all naked, bound upon a strong hackney, and his hands bound to-fore his breast. And every one of them held in his hands thorns wherewith they went beating him so sore that the blood trailed down more than in an hundred places on his body, but he said never a word.*

Anon Sir Bors went to rescue him that was his brother; and so he looked upon the other side of him, and saw a knight which brought a fair gentlewoman. And anon she espied where Sir Bors came riding. And when she came nigh him she deemed him a knight of the Round Table, whereof she hoped to have some comfort; and then she conjured him: "By the faith unto Him in whose service thou art entered in, and for the faith ye owe unto the high order of knighthood, and for the noble King Arthur's sake, that I suppose made thee knight, help me, and suffer me not to be shamed of this knight." When Bors heard her say thus he had so much sorrow there he knew not what to do. "For if I let my brother be in adventure he must be slain, and that would I not for all the earth. And if I help not the maid she is shamed forever, and also she shall lose her virginity the which she shall

young knight: "Sir, follow me." And anon he led him unto the Siege Perilous, beside Sir Launcelot; and the good man lifted up the cloth, and found there letters that said thus: This is the siege of Galahad, the haut prince. "Sir," said the old knight, "wit ye well that place is yours." And then he set him down surely in that siege. And then he said to the old man: "Sir, ye may now go your way, for well have ye done that ye were commanded to do; and recommend me unto my grandsire, King Pelles, and say him on my behalf, I shall come and see him as soon as ever I may." So the good man departed.

Then all the knights of the Table Round marvelled greatly of Sir Galahad, that he durst sit there in that Siege Perilous, and was so tender of age; and wist not from whence he came; and they said: "This is he by whom the Sangreal shall be enchieved." Then Sir Launcelot beheld his son and had great joy of him. [3] ✠

Here we arrive at the real beginning of the Quest. Everything that has gone before has been preparing the way for this – the dramatic appearance of the Grail and the coming of Galahad. At this point no one, except his mother and the mysterious hermit who brings him to the court, knows that the young knight in red armor is the son of Lancelot and Elaine of Carbonek. Once this is revealed it will be understood that the great knight has sired a child upon the Princess of the Grail, and that with his coming a new era will dawn in Camelot.

The Grail itself had been heralded and spoken about in whispers. Now it makes its startling appearance in the midst of the Round Table feast. It enters into a darkened hall, bringing light into a place of unknowing, and it reveals not only its own wonder and glory (though even that is veiled), but also that of the knights themselves, who are revealed unto each other in their true selves – "fairer than ever they saw afore" – for thus the Grail reveals us as we truly are, filled with the light of the spirit that is normally hidden within the veils of the flesh.

✠ *Then the king went home to Camelot, and so went to evensong to the great minster, and after that to supper, and every knight sat in his own place as they were before. Then anon they heard cracking and crying of thunder, that them thought the place should be destroyed. In the midst of this blast*

entered a sunbeam more clear by seven times than ever they saw day, and all there were alighted of the grace of the Holy Ghost. Then began every knight to behold other, and either saw other, by their seeming, fairer than ever they saw afore. There was no knight might speak one word a great while, and so they looked every man on other as they had been dumb. Then there entered into the hall the Holy Grail covered with white samite, but there was none might see it, nor who bare it. And there was all the hall filled with good odours, and every knight had such meats and drinks as he best loved in this world. And when the Holy Grail had been borne through the hall, then it departed suddenly, that they wist not where it went: then had they all breath to speak. And the king yielded thanks to God, of His good grace that he had sent them. "Certainly", said the king, "we ought to thank our Lord Jesu greatly for that he hath shewed us this day, at the reverence of this high feast of Pentecost." [4] ✠

When Merlin had ordained the Round Table he said, by them which should be fellows of the Round Table the truth of the Sangreal should well be known.

SIR THOMAS MALORY

Le Morte d'Arthur

The mystery of the Grail is such that few ever perceive it in the same way. Like a will-o'-the-wisp it dances before those who follow it, changing and shifting with each successive adventure. On one occasion Arthur himself was vouchsafed a vision of one of the Grail's most mysterious actions — its ability to change its shape. This was in order that all who came into its presence might feel more deeply the true wonder that lay at its heart. The five changes described below are only hinted at. Elsewhere in the same text are clues that suggest a sequence: from spear to cup to sword to stone to child. The first four changes reflect the form of four sacred objects — the "Hallows" or "Holy Things": the Lance of Longinus, used to piece the side of Christ and later on to strike the Dolorous Blow; the cup of the Last Supper; the sword of John the Baptist, with which the forerunner of Jesus was beheaded; and a mysterious Foundation Stone, which represents the land itself. The last change is emblematic of the Christian mystery of the sacrifice of innocent blood in the mystery of the Eucharist. These five shapes, assumed by the Grail, also equate with the five elements of spirit and matter: the Spear is fire; the Cup water; the Sword air; and the Stone earth; the fifth element which is soul or spirit completes the marvelous quincunx.

✠ *History tells us that in the land of King Arthur at this time, there was not a single chalice. The Grail appeared at the celebration of the mass in five different shapes, which no one ought to speak of because the secret things of the sacrament should not be spoken of. King Arthur beheld all the changes, the last of which was the change into a chalice. And the hermit that chanted the mass found under the altar cloth a document of instruction that declared that the body of our Lord God should be sacrificed in such a vessel. History does not say that there were no chalices elsewhere, but that there were none in all Great Britain and in the whole kingdom.* ✠

Thus it is revealed that the vision and sanctity of the Grail have been withheld from the kingdom of Logres until those are present who can achieve the tests that will equip them to succeed where all others have failed. Gawain, Arthur's nephew and one of the finest of the Round Table fellowship, is the first

to pledge himself to the Quest. But even as Gawain does so, the king realizes the full weight of Merlin's prophecy – that when the Grail appears the kingdom will be broken – for he knows that once the knights have set forth on the Quest, few of them will ever return. The underlying sadness of this overshadows the beginning of this highest endeavor, as it may well do in our own lives. Though we determine to set forth on our own search for inner truth, we may also be aware that the quest will change us forever. Many turn back at this point, unable to commit to the long and lonely path that lies before them. Only the knowledge of the healing that the Grail can offer keeps us on the path.

✠ *"Now," said Sir Gawaine, "we have been served this day of what meats and drinks we thought on; but one thing beguiled us, we might not see the Holy Grail, it was so preciously covered.*

✠

RIGHT: AN ILLUSTRATION OF THE KNIGHTS OF THE ROUND TABLE FROM A 15TH-CENTURY FRENCH MANUSCRIPT OF THE HISTORY OF THE HOLY GRAIL. THE STORY OF THE GRAIL FIRST APPEARED IN WRITTEN FORM IN FRANCE IN THE 12TH CENTURY AND WAS TOLD AND RETOLD OVER THE CENTURIES.

Onſiderãt q̃ par les triũphalles et glozieuſes oeuures que les vaillans hommes ⁊ nobles cheualiers anciennement firent en fait de cheualerie acquirent en leurs vi̇es louenges ⁊ gloire de perpetuelle me-

moire. Je voſtre treſhũble et treſobeiſſãt ſeruiteur a lhõneur ⁊ louẽge de vo'nõ treſredoubte ⁊ ſouuerain ſeigneʳ chief de toute nobleſſe ⁊ cheualerie. Charles huiti eſme de ce nõ treſcreſtiẽ roy de frãce. Affin q̃ voſtre cheualereux couraige ⁊ des ieu

Wherefore I will make here a vow, that tomorrow, without longer abiding, I shall labour in the quest of the Sangreal, that I shall hold me a twelve-month and a day, or more if need be, and never shall I return again unto the court till I have seen it more openly than it hath been seen here."

When they of the Table Round heard Sir Gawaine say so, they arose up the most part and made such avows as Sir Gawaine had made. Anon as King Arthur heard this he was greatly displeased, for he wist well they might not gainsay their vows. "Alas," said King Arthur unto Sir Gawaine, "ye have nigh slain me with the vow and promise that ye have made; for you have bereft me of the fairest fellowship and the truest of knighthood that ever were seen together in any realm of the world; for when they depart from hence I am sure they all shall never meet more in this world, for they shall die many in the quest. And I have loved them as well as my life, wherefore it shall grieve me right sore, the departure of this fellowship". [6]

Thus the knights are ready to depart on the Quest from which few will return; only three chosen men and one woman will succeed. Their journeys will be fraught with danger but also filled with wonder. The Grail will hover before them and show them the way to the realization of its mysteries. For this reason Arthur is saddened, for he

perceive it, the same is often true. We may be called upon to recognize and acknowledge our innermost self, that part of us that we tend to keep hidden, even from ourselves. The Grail quest teaches that in spite of all the obstacles encountered by the knights, the journey itself is as important as the end result. Even failure, such as that suffered by Lancelot and Gawain, has its lessons and is often no more than victory turned inside out. Perseverance and dedication are every bit as important as physical strength and courage; they can lead us to the experience of the Grail just as well and just as fittingly.

knows that never again will the whole fellowship of the Round Table meet together as they have this day. Their ways will take them into places where they will be forced to come to terms with the reality of their innermost being. Few will return, and those who do will be changed forever.

In our personal search for the Grail, in whatever form we

❖

ABOVE: THIS TAPESTRY BY TWO NOTABLE PRE-RAPHAELITE ARTISTS, SIR EDWARD BURNE-JONES AND WILLIAM MORRIS, GIVES A HIGHLY ROMANTIC VISION OF THE QUEST KNIGHTS. THE GALLANT KNIGHTS, ALL SPLENDIDLY MOUNTED AND READY TO EMBARK ON THEIR GREAT ADVENTURE, RECEIVE THEIR SWORDS, HELMETS, AND SHIELDS FROM THE HANDS OF ADORING MAIDENS.

Chapter Three

LANDS OF
WASTE AND WONDER

Certain themes dominate the story of the Quest. The ability of the Grail to bring about profound changes in those who seek it is one theme; another is the relationship of the Wounded King to the land over which he rules. Central to the tests and trials experienced by the knights is the ability to ask the meaning of a marvelous procession of holy objects – Hallows – that are carried through the hall of the Wounded King, the name applied to the Grail's guardian after the striking of the Dolorous Blow. For this wound, struck by Balin in self-defense, but with the sacred spear, will not heal. And, while it remains unhealed, the land over which the Grail King rules becomes a desert. It is known, thereafter, as the Waste Land, and nothing will grow there. All of this, we are told, can be reversed by the asking of a single question: Whom does the Grail serve? When Perceval blunders into the Castle of the Grail, he fails to ask that question. What he sees is perhaps too wonderful, and he is silenced by awe as much as by his inability to ask the question.

❦ *While they were talking of this and that, a squire entered, holding a white lance, and passed between the fire and those seated on the couch. All those present saw a drop of red blood run down from the tip of the white lance onto the squire's hand. The youth who had arrived that night watched this marvel but refrained from asking what it meant for fear of appearing rude. So he held his peace.*

Then two other squires came in, bearing candelabra of fine gold and niello work, and each candelabrum held at least ten candles. A damsel came in

---
❦

RIGHT: THE GRAIL MAY BE SEEN AS A SYMBOL FOR THE SPIRITUALITY IN OUR LIVES. UNTIL WE CAN ENQUIRE INTO OUR OWN SPIRITUALITY OUR LIVES WILL BE AS BARREN AS THE WASTE LAND OVER WHICH THE WOUNDED KING RULED.

with these squires, holding a grail. She was beautiful, gracious, splendidly dressed, and as she entered there was such a brilliant light that the candles lost their brightness, just as the stars do when the moon or the sun rises. Behind her came a damsel holding a silver carving platter. The grail that had preceded her was of refined gold, and it was set with the costliest and richest of precious stones that surpassed all other jewels. Like the squire with the lance, these damsels also passed before the couch and entered another chamber.

The youth watched them pass, but he did not dare to ask concerning the grail and whom one served with it.[1]

Wonders of this kind are not limited to stories. We ourselves are countries of the spirit, in which many marvelous things are to be found. It is only our failure to inquire more deeply into the nature of our own spirituality that prevents us from realizing the vision of the Grail in our lives. Like the Wounded King, our relationship to the land of our being can be damaged by a failure to deal with the truth when it manifests in our lives, with the result that we too suffer from the "Waste Land" effect, the drying up of the soul, and the loss of spiritual vitality. It is with the promise of the Grail that this process can be reversed, that healing and restoration can come to the inner as well as the outer Waste Land.

The special relationship of the king to the country over which he ruled first comes to our attention in the myths of the Celtic people. There, if the king is in any way imperfect in body – such as the hero who loses a hand in battle – he must give up his kingship. In the Grail tradition, modern as well as ancient, this reflects a need for the state of woundedness to be acknowledged, for only thus can healing begin.

LEFT: IN THIS PAINTING BY ARTHUR HUGHES (1832–1915), GALAHAD IS GUIDED BY ANGELS AS HE SETS OUT ON HIS SACRED QUEST.

The Grail is a stone of the purest kind ... called *lapsit exillas* ... There never was human so ill but that if he one day sees that stone, he cannot die within the week that follows.

WOLFRAM VON ESCHENBACH:

Parzival

The causes for the Waste Land are not always ascribed to the Dolorous Blow. Other, more ancient reasons are sometimes given. In the passage that follows, we see that a great wrong can also bring about a deeper wounding than that of a blow, and that the land suffers dryness in much the same way that the human spirit can become dried up if the healing waters of love and truth are

forgotten or neglected. Here, it is the feminine heart of the land, rather than its masculine counterpart, that is wounded. Yet even here there is the promise of healing. The Waste Land, brought about through the misplaced desires of King Amangons, will also flower again, and the mysterious court of the Rich Fisherman — another aspect of the Wounded King — awaits discovery. Once again the pattern is of wounding and wasting, but with the promise of healing and restoration to come.

In this story we learn of the Maidens of the Wells, women who offer service and hospitality to all weary travelers who come their way. But the sustenance they offer is more than mere comfort; it is spiritual food and drink. Thus when those who offer these gifts are attacked and wounded, the gifts are withdrawn and the land suffers. It becomes a Waste Land, which can only be healed by the coming of the Grail and the restoration of the Maidens. This deep and moving story is less

ABOVE LEFT: A QUEST KNIGHT ARMED AND READY TO DO BATTLE. BUT A KNIGHT NEEDED MORE THAN MERE PHYSICAL COURAGE; HE ALSO NEED SPIRITUAL STRENGTH TO FACE THE DEMANDS AND CHALLENGES OF THE QUEST.

familiar than many of those associated with the Grail. It is nonetheless important for the description it gives us of a magical place where wounds can be healed, and where the seeking of a place – the court of the Rich Fisherman – is an action that can restore the dried-up soul as it restores the dried-up Waste Land of the story.

Whenever a traveler came upon one of the wells and asked for food and drink, a fair damsel would appear from the well bearing a cup of gold with meats, pastries, and bread; another damsel would bring a white napkin and a dish of gold or silver with the food he had asked for. If the food did not please the traveler, different food, more to his liking, would be brought to him. The Maidens of the Wells joyfully and graciously served any wayfarer who came to the well for food.

The evil and craven-hearted King Amangons was the first to break the custom, and thereafter many others followed his example. It was the king's duty to maintain and protect the damsels, but he forced himself upon one of the damsels and, to her great sorrow, did away with her maidenhead and carried off her golden cup. From then on the damsel did not serve travelers who asked for food from the well, and all the other damsels served in such a way that no one would see them.

When the king's vassals learned that their king forced himself upon the damsel he desired, they also forced themselves upon the other damsels and carried off their cups of gold. From then on no damsel came forth from the wells to serve travelers. Because of this, the land began to decline and the king and all those who had harmed the damsels met with an evil end. The kingdom was laid waste as trees lost their leaves, meadows and flowers died, and the waters dried up. No one could find the Court of the Rich Fisherman that used to make in the land a glittering glory of gold and silver, of ermine and miniver, of rich palls of silk, of meats and stuffs, of gentle falcons and merlins and tercels and sparrow-hawks and falcons peregrine.[2] *

The adventures experienced by the Quest knights were very much of a piece. They are really exemplars of the need for spiritual grace, of certain qualities that lead inward to the country of the spirit. Not all are able to succeed, and of those who do not, some fail gloriously – none more so than Lancelot and Gawain, two of the foremost heroes of Arthur's court, but each one fatally flawed. Lancelot, who loves Arthur's queen, fails precisely because he loves Guinevere more than the Quest. Gawain, who is a worldly man, experiences many of the greatest trials of the search and overcomes most. In the end, he is excluded because he seems to lose heart, or perhaps because he is in reality seeking something other than the Grail.

In the passages that follow we see two moments from the long and arduous journeys of these two men. Beginning with Lancelot, we see him come face to face with the heart of the mystery, only to be turned away. In this part of the story, the great knight has already traveled far and experienced a variety of adventures. Yet, try as he might, the essential mystery of the Grail continues to elude him. Here, he comes closer than ever he has before.

✠ *Lancelot kept on until he reached a room with a locked door, which he tried in vain to open. Then he heard a voice*

— ✠ —

RIGHT: LANCELOT AT THE CHAPEL OF THE HOLY GRAIL BY SIR EDWARD BURNE-JONES. THE SIGHT OF THE GRAIL HAS LEFT LANCELOT IN A SWOON, UNABLE TO MOVE OR TO SPEAK.

chanting so sweetly that it seemed to be the voice of some heavenly creature. The voice sang, "Glory, praise, and honor to you, Father in heaven!" When Lancelot heard what the voice was saying, his heart melted and he knelt beside the door, for he thought that the Holy Grail might be inside. He said, weeping, "Fair sweet Father Jesus Christ, if I ever did anything that pleased you, do not bear me any grudge, but show me some revelation of what I am seeking."

As soon as Lancelot had said this, he saw the door open and through it there shone a light so bright that it seemed the sun itself was in the room. He was so happy and felt such desire to see where this brightness came from that he forgot everything else. He was about to enter when a voice said to him, "Flee, Lancelot, do not enter, for you will regret it." Lancelot drew back sorrowfully, still wanting to enter but heeding the warning.

But he looked into the room and saw the Holy Vessel covered with a red silk cloth. All around were angels serving the Holy Vessel, some holding silver censers and lighted candles, other holding crosses and altar vessels. An old man dressed like a priest sat in front of the Holy Vessel and appeared to be assisting at the sacrament of the mass. When he was about to elevate the host, there appeared in the air the figures of three men, two of whom placed the youngest

of them in the priest's hands. And thus he raised him on high and appeared to show him to the people.

Lancelot was astonished to see these things. The priest seemed to be so burdened with the figure he held up that Lancelot wished to go to his aid, since none of the others present were lending a hand. His desire was so great that he forgot the warning not to enter the room. He went to the door, saying, "Father Jesus Christ, do not punish me for my wish to help this worthy man." Then he went in and walked toward the silver table. As he approached it, he felt a breath of air as hot as if it was mixed with flame, and it hit him fiercely in the face. His strength failed him and all his limbs were powerless. Then he felt several hands seize and carry him away; they cast him out of the room and deserted him there.

The next morning the people of the palace arose to find Lancelot lying before the chamber door, and they wondered what had happened. When they bid him rise and he showed no sign of hearing them and did not stir, they thought he was dead. They removed his armor and examined him, and found he was alive but could not speak or move. They picked him up and carried him into one of the rooms and laid him on a bed far from the crowd, so that he would not be disturbed. They took care of him

as best they could, remaining by his side all day and speaking to him to see if he would reply. But he never said a word. They examined his pulse and thought it very strange that a knight who was fully alive could not speak to them. Some said that perhaps it was some vengeance or manifestation of Our Lord.[3] ✠

Lancelot recovers, but it is left to son, Galahad, to achieve what his father cannot.

For Gawain, the experience is somewhat different. Wounded and wearied from combat, he takes his ease in a castle, which he fails to recognize as belonging to the Grail King. What follows is a salutary lesson that only someone with Gawain's noble soul could survive. Having arrived at a castle that, at first hand, seems no different from all the others at which he has claimed shelter on his long journey, Gawain soon begins to perceive that this is not like any other place where he has been, and that it offers a new kind of challenge. First he does battle with a powerful assailant

---

✠

ABOVE: SIR GAWAIN KNEELING AT A FOUNTAIN, FROM A 15TH-CENTURY FRENCH MANUSCRIPT. DESPITE HIS SINCERE EFFORTS TO ACHIEVE THE GRAIL, THIS WORLDLY KNIGHT IS DESTINED TO FAIL IN HIS QUEST.

who wounds him and is wounded in turn. Both men lie stunned. Then comes a series of events that are typical of the experience of the Grail knights, except that here Gawain's punishment for failure is more extreme than most.

❧ While Sir Gawain lay on the couch with the knight near him, the palace began to shake; there was terrible thunder and lightning but no rain. Sir Gawain was dismayed, but he was so tired that he could not lift his head, and his brain was so confused with the thunder claps that he did not know if it were day or night.

Then a sweet, soft breeze swept through the hall, and there came the sound of many sweet voices singing, "Glory, and praise, and honor unto the king of heaven!" And the sweetest of perfumes filled the hall.

The voices sounded so beautiful to Sir Gawain that he thought they were not of this earth. When he opened his eyes and saw nothing, he knew they were no earthly voices. He wanted to rise but could not do so since he had lost the power to move.

Then he saw coming from a chamber the damsel who had previously borne the Holy Vessel before the table. In front of her came two tapers and two censers. When she came to the middle of the palace she laid the Holy Grail on a table of silver. Sir Gawain saw ten censers giving forth perfume and all the sweet voices began to sing, "Blessed be the father of heaven."

When the song had lasted a long time, the damsel took the vessel and carried it into the chamber she had come from. The voices were silent and all the windows opened and then closed, and the hall grew so dark that Sir Gawain could see nothing. He became aware that he felt healthy and whole again and that the wound in his right shoulder was healed. He arose joyfully and went to seek the knight who had fought with him, but could not find him.

Then he heard the sound of people approaching and felt them lay hold of him and carry him from the hall and bind him to a cart in the middle of the court. With that he fell asleep.

Sir Gawain awoke in the morning to find he was lying in a vile cart and his shield was bound onto the shaft in front of him and his horse was tied behind the cart, while in the shaft was a thin and meager horse. He felt deeply shamed to find himself in such a sad state, and he wished he were dead.

A damsel came toward him bearing a whip, and she began to hit the horse and to lead it through the streets of the forth in search of adventure, he arrived almost at once at the Castle of the Grail and witnessed the Grail procession through the hall. But on the advice of well-meaning helpers he failed to ask the all-important question that would have set in motion the healing of both the Wounded King and the Waste Land. As those who set forth upon their own quest for healing so often do, he failed to act, to begin the soul's journey to peace. But Perceval's failure left room for another great figure – Galahad, the son of Lancelot du Lac, the greatest hero to sit at the Round Table.

We have already heard something of the circumstances of Galahad's birth; his coming is equally mysterious and foreshadows the wondrous events that are about to occur.

....

ere is the book of thy descent:
Here begins the Book of the Sangreal,
Here begin the terrors,
Here begin the miracles

The Quest del Saint Graal

....

So the king and all went unto the court, and every knight knew his own

place, and set him therein, and young men that were knights served them.

So when they were served, and all sieges filled save only the Siege Perilous, anon there befell a marvellous adventure, that all the doors and windows of the palace shut by themselves. Then the hall was greatly darked; and therewith they were all abashed. Then King Arthur spake first and said: "By God, fair fellows and lords, we have seen this day marvels, but before night I suppose we shall see greater."

In the meanwhile came in a good old man, clothed all in white, and there was no one knew from whence he came. And with him he brought a young knight, in red arms, without sword or shield, save a scabbard hanging by his side. And these words he said: "Peace be with you, fair lords." Then the old man said unto Arthur: "Sir, I bring here a young knight, of king's lineage, and of the kindred of Joseph of Aramathie, whereby the marvels of this court, and of strange realms, shall be fully accomplished..."

The king was right glad of his words, and said unto the good man: "Sir, ye be right welcome, and the young knight with you." Then the old man made the young man to unarm him, and he was in a coat of red sendal, and bare a mantle upon his shoulder that was furred with ermine, and put that upon him. And the old knight said unto the

never get again." Then lifted he up his eyes and said, weeping: "Fair sweet Lord Jesu Christ, whose liege man I am, keep Lionel, my brother, that these knights slay him not, and for pity of you, and for Mary's sake, I shall succour this maid." [5]

The result of this test is painful in every way. Bors' decision to help the lady in distress proves to be no more than a false lead, for she is an enchantress sent to distract him from the course of the Quest. He must also work hard to repair the

damage done to his relationship with Lionel. It is typical of the kind of trials which the Quest knights must face that their decisions are often, humanly speaking, wrong, although they are made with the best of intentions.

Indeed, these are but a handful of the endlessly varied trials undergone by the knights. Few are found to have the qualities necessary to achieve the full mystery of the Grail. Yet even those who do not succeed are changed and ennobled by the experience. We also, who set out on our own inner search, may well find the way blocked by aspects of our selves that arise only when we have begun the process of the Quest. One of the most important effects that the Grail can have upon us is to foster an ability to face such realizations squarely so that we become strengthened thereby and are finally enabled to push beyond the temporary setbacks that confront us. This is true of all journeys undertaken in pursuit of soul-health and well-being. The Grail Quest above all promises that, as we are tested, so shall we achieve greater access to the Mystery.

LEFT: THIS 14TH-CENTURY ILLUSTRATION FROM THE QUETE DU SAINT GRAAL ET LA MORT D'ARTHUS VIVIDLY DEPICTS SIR BORS' DILEMMA. WILL HE RESCUE HIS BROTHER LIONEL, OR SUCCUMB TO THE CHARMS OF THE ENCHANTRESS?

C h a p t e r F o u r

THE QUEST DEEPENS

When they set forth in Quest of the Grail, the knights had little idea what they would be facing. Used to adventures that involved magic and the rescue of distressed women, they were unprepared for the spiritual nature of the trials they now encountered. At the beginning they rode together in companies of four or five, but gradually, as the roads divided, they went their ways alone. At sea or on land, they wandered for year after year, following wherever their horses or the whims of fate led them. They met many strange and wondrous things, saw strange and miraculous visions, encountered enemies and friends whose words would often change the path they took forever. But ever before them hovered the image of the Grail, emitting light that illumined the soul. Perceval, above all, having failed to ask the all-important question, was forced to follow a circuitous path in search of the elusive Grail Castle and its Wounded King. Sometimes, as in the next passage, he encountered people who were caught in the mysterious enchantments that lay over the land of Logres, and who waited, just as the Fisher King himself waited, for an act that would eventually bring them release.

The Grail Knight, distant,
wrought of clay
Dreams of a King whose
wounds will never heal
Unless the Cup is brought to earth.

JOHN MATTHEWS

The Mysteries of the Grail

Perceval was so far from land that he could see nothing but sea. The ship sailed on, guided by God, until they saw a castle and an island. As they came near the castle, they saw four bell ringers dressed in white sounding the bells at the four corners of the town.

As soon as the ship had taken haven under the castle, the sea withdrew and the ship was left on dry land. Perceval, his horse, and the pilot left the ship and approached the castle, and found there the most beautiful halls and mansions they had ever seen. He looked under a tall tree and found a fountain surrounded by rich pillars and gravel that seemed to be made of gold and precious stones. Two men were sitting above the fountain; their hair was white although their faces seemed young. When they saw Perceval they bowed down and worshiped his shield and kissed the cross. They said they had known another knight who had worn this shield; they had seen him before Christ was crucified. Perceval marveled at this because they were talking of a time long ago.

"Lords, what was his name?" asked Perceval.

The masters answered, "Joseph of Arimathea, but there was no cross on the shield before the death of Jesus Christ. He had it set on the shield after the crucifixion for the sake of the Savior he loved so well."

ABOVE: DURING THE COURSE OF THE QUEST THE KNIGHTS WERE PARTED AND FOLLOWED THEIR OWN PATHS, ENCOUNTERING STRANGE VISIONS AND MARVELLOUS ADVENTURES THAT ADDED AN UNLOOKED FOR SPIRITUAL DIMENSION TO THEIR LONG JOURNEY.

When Perceval took off his shield, one of the men set before it a beautiful posy of flowering herbs. Perceval looked past the fountain and saw a round vessel that look like ivory and it was so large that there was an armed knight within. He spoke to the knight but he would not answer. Perceval asked the good masters who this knight was, but they said it was not the time for him to know. They led him to a great hall, carrying his shield before him, where they worshiped it. The hall was richer and finer than any he had seen, and in the middle of the hall was an image of the Savior with his apostles. The galleries were full of people who seemed to be of great holiness; and they were, or otherwise they would not have been able to stay there.

The masters told Perceval that this was the royal hall. Perceval had never seen such a rich hall, for there were tables of gold and ivory. One of the masters clapped his hands and 33 men entered the hall; they were clad in white and each one had a red cross in the *middle of his breast. They worshiped before the Savior, set out their cups, washed themselves in a golden laver, and seated themselves at table. Perceval was invited to join the masters at their table. There they were gloriously served, but Perceval was more interested in looking around him than in eating.*

Then Perceval saw a golden chain come down from above him, loaded with precious jewels and a crown of gold. The chain descended a great length and was supported by nothing but the power of Our Lord. When the masters saw the rope descend they opened a wide pit in the middle of the hall. A great cry issued forth from the pit – a cry more sorrowful than any Perceval had ever heard. When the men heard it, they stretched out their hands toward Heaven and all began to weep. Perceval wondered what this sorrow might be. He saw the chain of gold descend into the pit and it stayed there until they had eaten. Then it drew itself into the air again and went aloft. Perceval did not know what became of it, and the masters covered the pit again, and it was pitiful to hear the voices that issued from within.[1] ✠

✠

ABOVE LEFT: AS ARTHUR'S KNIGHTS FOLLOWED THEIR QUEST FOR THE GRAIL, MANY TEMPT-ATIONS WERE THRUST IN THEIR PATH IN AN EFFORT TO LEAD THEM ASTRAY. HERE PERCEVAL DINES WITH A MAIDEN WHO IS INTENT ON SEDUCING HIM.

The mysterious people, imprisoned within the earth, who daily give voice to their anguish, are metaphors of the human soul, shut up and betrayed by its own nature. Like the Wounded King, this nameless host await the coming of the one who will set them free, who will ask the Grail question. They are the servants of the Grail, the families of knights who have guarded the sacred vessel through the ages, and who have not been set free. Like the Wounded King himself, they are trapped by their inability to act. Only the coming of the promised seeker, the one who will activate the healing agency of the sacred vessel, can offer them the chance to move on.

For those engaged in the Quest, the experience was different, in that help was always at hand. Despite the pitfalls that awaited them around every corner, as they journeyed through the vast forests of Logres, if one of them experienced something that puzzled him, one of the friendly hermits who lived in the depths of the woods would be on hand to interpret the dream, spell out the true meaning of the vision, and explicate the adventures in all their rich and colorful symbolism.

Lancelot, forever forbidden, it seems, to come close to the mystery he sought with all the power of his great soul, was more than once vouchsafed a vision that answered the questions of his heart, but which he failed to understand. In this passage he reaches a crossroads that is symbolic of the spiritual impasse in his Quest and an actual turning of the ways. A hermit is there to tell him the meaning of his vision; and although the hermit has little hope to offer the great knight,

family itself. But this is not enough to get him closer to the Grail. Only his own spirituality can do that. We ourselves, stumbling like Lancelot on the threshold of the great mystery, often fail to understand it. If we are lucky, there are those on hand who can help us tease out the true meaning of the experience. If not, or if we disregard the help of others, we may find ourselves with a longer, harder path to follow.

✠ *Then Sir Launcelot rode till that he came to a Cross, and took that for his host for that night. And so he put his horse to pasture, and took off his helm and his shield, and made his prayers unto the Cross that he never fall in deadly sin again. And so he laid him down to sleep. And anon as he was asleep it befell him in a vision, that there came a man afore him surrounded with stars, and the man had a crown of gold on his head, and led in his fellowship seven kings and two knights. And all these worshipped the Cross, kneeling upon their knees, holding up their hands toward the heaven. And they all said:*

✠

ABOVE LEFT: AFTER SEEING A VISION IN HIS SLEEP, LANCELOT SEEKS COUNSEL FROM A HERMIT WHO EXPLAINS THAT THE VISION DENOTES HIS LINEAGE AND DESCENT FROM THE GRAIL FAMILY.

he does, in the process, tell us more about the long lineage of the family who have been entrusted with the guardianship of the sacred vessel. Lancelot himself, and Galahad after him, are related to Joseph of Arimathea, and thus to the Grail

"Fair sweet Father of heaven, come and visit us, and yield unto us all that we have deserved."

Then looked Launcelot up to the heaven, and it seemed the clouds did open, and an old man came down, with a company of angels, and alighted among them, and gave unto everyone his blessing, and called them his servants, and good and true knights. And when this old man had said thus he came to one of those knights, and said: "I have lost all that I have set in thee, for though thou hast ruled thee against me as a warrior, and used wrong wars with vainglory, more for the pleasure of the world than to please me, therefore thou shalt be confounded."

All this vision saw Sir Launcelot at the Cross. And on the morn he took his horse and rode till midday and by adventure he met an hermit, and each of them saluted the other; and there he rested with that good man all night. Then said the good man unto Launcelot: "Of whence be ye?" "Sir," said he, "I am of Arthur's court, and my name is Sir Launcelot du Lake that am in the quest of the Sangreal, and therefore I pray you to counsel me of a vision the which I had at the Cross." And so he told him all.

"Lo, Sir Launcelot," said the good man, "thus thou might understand the high lineage that thou art come of, which thine vision betokeneth. After the passion of Jesu Christ forty year, Joseph of Aramathie preached to King Evelake. And of the seven kings and the two knights whom you saw; the first of them

---

ABOVE: THE QUEST FOR THE GRAIL IS A SPIRITUAL JOURNEY OF DISCOVERY. HERE LANCELOT'S COMPANIONS HEAR MASS BEFORE EMBARKING UPON THE NEXT STAGE OF THEIR QUEST.

is called Nappus, an holy man; and the
second is called Nacien, in remembrance
of his grandsire; and the third was called
Helias le Grose; and the fourth Lisais;
and the fifth Jonas. And of him came
King Launcelot thy grandsire, the which
wedded the king's daughter of Ireland,
and he was as worthy a man as thou art,
and of him came King Ban, thy father,
the which was the last of the seven kings.
And by thee, Sir Launcelot, it signifieth
that the angels said thou were none of
the seven fellowships. And the last was
the ninth knight, he was signified to a
lion, for he should pass all manner of
earthly knights, that is Sir Galahad, the
which thou gat on King Pelles' daughter;
and thou ought to thank God more than
any other man living, for of a sinner
earthly thou hast no peer as in
knighthood, nor never shall be. But little
thanks hast thou given to God for all the
great virtues that God hath lent thee."
"Sir," said Launcelot," ye say that that
good knight is my son." "That oughtest
thou to know and no man better," said
the good man, "for thou knewest the
daughter of King Pelles fleshly, and on
her thou begattest Galahad, and that
was he that at the feast of Pentecost sat
in the Siege Perilous." "Well," said
Launcelot, "meseemeth that good knight
should pray for me unto the High Father,
that I fall not to sin again." "Trust thou
well," said the good man, "thou farest

mickle the better for his prayer; but the
son shall not bear the wickedness of the
father, nor the father bear the wickedness
of the son, but each shall bear his own
burden. And therefore beseek thou only
God, and He will help thee in all thy
needs." And then Sir Launcelot and he
went to supper, and so laid him to rest.
And so on the morn he heard his mass and
took his arms, and so took his leave. [2]

Let not him who seeks
cease until he finds,
and when he finds
he shall be astonished.

THE GOSPEL OF THOMAS

The origins of the story of the
Grail remain mysterious, as indeed
it should, since to show forth all
the hidden mystery of any great
wonder is to rob it of some of its
power to move and enlighten us.
Only in the work of the German
poet Wolfram von Eschenbach are
there hints and clues that point to
an even more ancient history than
we might suppose – a history that
begins in the East. It is certainly
possible that the knights who
went on Crusade to the Holy
Lands found and brought back the
seeds of this wondrous story, as

suggested here. But there is still a deeper mystery – for behind one version lies another, still older version that can be read in the patterns of the stars.

✠ *For Kiot of old, the master whom men spake of in days of yore,*

Far off in Toledo's city, found in Arabic writ the lore

By men cast aside and forgotten, the tale of the wondrous Grail;

But first must he learn the letters, nor black art might there avail.

By the grace of baptismal waters, by the light of our Holy Faith,

He read the tale, else 'twere hidden; for never, the story saith,

Might heathen skill have shown us the virtue that hidden lies

In this mighty Grail, or Its marvels have opened to Christian eyes.

'Twas a heathen, Flegetanis, who had won for his wisdom fame,

And saw many a wondrous vision, (From Israel's race he came,

And the blood of the kings of old-time, of Solomon did he share,)

He wrote in the days long vanished, ere we as a shield might bear

The cross of our Holy baptism 'gainst the craft and the wiles of Hell,

And he was the first of earth's children the lore of the Grail to tell.

By his father's side a heathen, a calf he for God did hold,

How wrought the devil such folly, on a folk so wise, of old?

And the highest Who knoweth all wonders, why stretched He not forth His Hand

To the light of His truth to turn them? For who may His power withstand!

And the heathen, Flegetanis, could read in the heavens high

How the stars roll on their courses, how they circle the silent sky,

And the time when their wandering endeth — and the life and the lot of men

He read in the stars, and strange secrets he saw, and he spake again

Low, with bated breath and fearful, of the thing that is called the grail,

In a cluster of stars was it written, the name, nor their lore shall fail.

And he quoth thus, "A host of angels this marvel to earth once bore,

But too pure for earth's sin and sorrow the heaven they sought once more,

And the sons of baptized men hold It, and guard It with humble heart,

And the best of mankind shall those knights be who have in such service part."

Then Kiot my master read this, the tale Flegetanis told,

And he sought for the name of the people, in Latin books of old,

Who of God were accounted worthy

for this wondrous Grail to care,

Who were true and pure in their
dealings and a lowly heart might bear.

And in Britain, and France, and
Ireland thro' the chronicles he sought

Till at length, in the land of Anjou,
the story to light was brought.

There, in true and faithful record,
was written of Mazadan,

And the heroes, the sons of his body,
and further the story ran,

How Titurel, the grandsire, left his
kingdom to Frimutel,

And at length to his son, Anfortas,
the grail and its heirdom fell:

That his sister was Herzeleide, and
with Gamuret she wed

And bare him for a son the hero
whose wanderings ye now have read.[3] 🜚

Like his peers, Gawain found his way again and again to the threshold of the mystery, only to be turned away. Yet here, in a rare episode, he seems to succeed – not wholly, and not finally, but with enough power to set free some of those caught up in the power of the Grail, and to bring praise upon his own head.

Arriving once again at the Castle of the Grail, he observes the procession of the Hallows. But there are differences here, and once again the outcome is variable. We are presented again with the sorrow of the Wounded King's companions, and we see that when Gawain asks the question, the result is a dramatic healing, a release of souls long held in thrall. Yet even now the Quest is not over; Gawain is gifted with a sword and is instructed not to put too much trust in material objects, but to rely on the armor and weapons of the spirit. This advice applies to many of our own life-tests.

🜚 *The four who bore spear and salver drew near and laid the spear upon the table and the salver beneath it. Then Gawain saw a great marvel, for the spear shed three drops of blood into the salver that was beneath. The old man, the host, took them away. The maiden placed a beautiful vessel containing bread on the table. The old man broke it into three and ate.*

Gawain could no longer contain himself and said, "My host, please tell me what this great company and these marvels mean." As he spoke, all the people, knights and ladies alike, sprang from their seats with the sound of great rejoicing. The host bade them to be seated and make no sound.

"Sir Gawain," he said, "this marvel is from God and may not be known to all. But since you asked, sweet kinsman and dear guest, I may not withhold the truth. It is the Grail that you behold. You have won the world's praise for your manhood and your courage in achieving this difficult Quest. I will say no more of the Grail except that great happiness has come from your question. Many who had little hope of deliverance are now set free from the sorrow they have borne. We all had great confidence that Perceval would learn the secret of the Grail, but he departed as a coward who ventured nothing and asked nothing. Therefore, his Quest was a failure and he did not learn what he should have learned. He could have freed many from hardship who live and yet are dead. This misfortune befell because of the strife of kinsmen, when one brother fought the other for his land. For that treason the wrath of God was visited on him and all his kin, and all were lost.

"That was a woeful fate, for the living were driven out, but the dead must abide in the semblance of life and suffer bitter sorrow. Yet they had hope that with God's grace they should come to the end of their grief, in such a manner as I shall tell you.

"A man could end their sorrow by demanding to know the truth of these marvels; thus would their penance be fulfilled and they would again be joyful. Both the dead and the living now give thanks to God and to you, for because of you they are now released. This spear and this food nourish me and no one else, for I was guiltless of the deed, so God did not condemn me. I am dead but

I do not bear the semblance of death, and these my people are also dead. Although all knowledge is not ours, yet we have plenty of riches and know no lack. But these maidens are not dead, and they have no other penance except that they are where I am. It is by the command of God that they nourish me once a year. Know this, that the adventures you have seen have come from the Grail, and your Quest has ended the penance."

He gave Gawain the sword, saying he was well armed because, however much he used it in strife, it would never break. He bade him wear it all his days. Thus he ended his tale and told Gawain he might now end his Quest. And concerning the maidens, it was because of their unstained purity that God had entrusted them with the service of the Grail. Now that their task was ended, they were sad at heart, for they knew never again would the Grail be so openly seen, now that Sir Gawain had learned its secrets. It was by the grace of God that mortal eyes could behold it, and its mysteries henceforth no tongue would tell.

When the day began to dawn and the old man had finished his tale, he vanished, and with him went the Grail and all the company. All that remained in the hall were the three knights and the maidens. [4]

Success and failure were hard to judge in the bewildering and constantly shifting pattern of the Quest. The light of the Grail continued to beckon, and in time there was only one road to follow, only one way that led to transformation and renewal. Just as the knights set forth together, only to separate as the ways divided, so, as the Quest drew toward its close, fewer and fewer paths were offered, fewer and fewer ways presented themselves to the seekers. Drawn ever onward by the power of the search, the few knights who remained were made ready for a final, shattering climax – the achievement of the Grail itself.

Until this point, as so often in our own lives, the Quest itself had been almost more important than its final outcome. Now this changed. The experiences that had gone before were all seen to lead toward this single point, a focused moment that would take the Quest knights into and beyond the mystery of the Grail.

ABOVE LEFT: THE WORLDLY GAWAIN, HERE DEPICTED SETTING OFF TO FOLLOW LANCELOT, WAS DESTINED NOT TO ACHIEVE THE GRAIL. OVERLEAF: SIR LANCELOT LIFTS THE STONE OFF HIS OWN PREDESTINED GRAVE AND LEARNS ABOUT HIS NAME AND HIS PARENTAGE.

C h a p t e r   F i v e

ACHIEVEMENT

The final chapters of the Quest are breathless with a sense of expectancy. Wonder follows wonder, adventure leads into adventure, in an almost seamless garment of words and images. The fulfillment of long-awaited deeds fills one with a sense of vast forces moving toward a conclusion that has been foretold from a time long before the age of Arthur. Which is indeed the case, since the story really begins with the beginning of time, when the elements of Creation itself were mixed in a great crater or mixing bowl by the gods, and the stars and worlds poured forth from the sacred vessel that will one day be called the Grail. This part of its history has still to be written, yet it is there, for all to see, if we consider deeply enough.

On the Quest the three knights and the sister of Perceval voyage together in a mysterious boat, which leads them at length to another craft, one that had been created, long ages since, for this very purpose. Built at the command of the biblical King Solomon, this ship contains treasures of spiritual power and grace. It is a fitting vehicle to convey the Quest knights in the final part of their own momentous journey, just as, for those of us today who set forth on just such a voyage, the story itself may become a spiritual craft that can take us from our own inner harbor to places of deep wonder and renewal.

In the part of the story from which the following extract comes, the three Quest knights have disembarked from their own vessel and, having met with Dindrane (here called, simply, "the damsel"), are about to go aboard the mystical Ship of Solomon. The allegorical and symbolic references (very Christianized in this

---

✠

RIGHT: THREE DAMSELS WATCH AS A SHIP SETS SAIL WITH THE HOLY TREASURE, A METAPHOR FOR THE SPIRITUAL JOURNEY OF LIFE.

instance) that follow are an example of the kind of mystical imagery that threads the Grail texts through and through. Thus the ship itself is "Faith," and here too we read of yet another cause of the Waste Land — pride, a cause of so much pain and suffering, then as now. On this magical vessel, as so often in our own journeys, every object has a deeper meaning. It is more than just itself; it is pierced through with a numinous reality that transcends the ordinary. Those who take up the Quest for themselves should expect to find many such points of reference on the way, whether they are simply reading about the journeys of the knights or following their own path.

"Fair lords," the damsel said, "in yonder ship lies the adventure for which Our Lord has brought you together; you must leave this ship and go to that one." So they disembarked and made their way to the other ship, which was more magnificent than the one they had left. But they were amazed to find no one there. On the side of the ship they found words written in Chaldean that spelled out an awful and mysterious warning to anyone who entered it. It read: "Before you enter me, whoever you are, be sure

you are full of faith and without blemish, for I am nothing if not faith and belief. As soon as you desert your faith, I will desert you."

When they had read these words, the damsel said to Perceval, "Do you know who I am?"

"No," he replied, "I have never seen you before."

"I am your sister and the daughter of King Pelles. I have revealed myself to you so that you may better believe what I have to say. If you do not believe perfectly in Jesus Christ, you should not enter this ship, for you shall perish. The ship is such a precious thing that no one with any evil vice can stay in it with impunity."

Upon hearing this, Perceval saw that she was indeed his sister and showed her his happiness. He said, "Certainly, fair sister, I will enter. If I lack faith, may I perish as a disloyal man; and if I am full of faith, such as a knight should be, may I be saved."

"Enter with confidence," she said, "and may Our Lord be your protection and defense."

While she was saying this, Galahad crossed himself and went on board, and the damsel followed him. Seeing this, the other also went on board. They examined the ship and said they did not think there was ever such a fine vessel. In the body of the ship, they found a precious

ABOVE: ARTHUR AND HIS COMPANIONS ABOARD A
SHIP. A SHIP APPEARS THROUGHOUT THE GRAIL
QUEST AS A SYMBOLIC REFERENCE FOR FAITH,
ONE OF MANY SUCH ALLEGORICAL IMAGES.

cloth stretched like a curtain and
beneath it a large, fine couch.

Galahad raised the cloth and saw the
most beautiful couch he had ever seen.
At the head was a beautiful crown of
gold, and at the foot a shining sword
lying across the couch and drawn half a
foot from its scabbard.

The sword had various peculiarities.
The pommel was formed of stones of
every color, each with a virtue of its
own. The hilt was formed from the bones
of two different beasts. One was from a
type of serpent called the "papalustes"
that dwells only in Scotland; anyone
who holds any of its bones need have no
fear of feeling excessive heat. The other
bone was from a medium-sized fish
called the "ostenax" that lives only in the
Euphrates River; anyone who has one of

these bones will have no recollection of
any other joy or pain except the one that
prompted him to seize this bone. But as
soon as he puts it down, his memory will
function again as usual. The two bones
were covered with vermilion cloth and
inscribed with these words: "I am
marvelous to see and know. For no man
has ever been able to grasp me, save one;
and this one shall surpass in skill all
who have been before him or who shall
come after him."

When they had read this inscription,
Perceval tried to grasp the sword but
failed. Then Bors stretched forth his
hand, but to no effect. They said to
Galahad, "Sir, try this sword. For we
know you can achieve what others have
failed to do." But he said he would not
try, "For I see greater marvels here than I
have ever seen before." He examined the
blade that was partly drawn from the
scabbard and he saw more letters, red as
blood. They said: "Let no one be so bold
as to draw me from the scabbard unless
he can fight more boldly than anyone
else. Whoever draws me out must know
that he will soon be dead or injured.
And this has already been proved once."

The damsel told them what had
happened not long ago. A ship arrived at
the kingdom of Logres when there was a
war between King Lambar and King
Varlan. One day King Lambar and King
Varlan had assembled their hosts on the

coast where the ship had arrived, and King Varlan had been defeated. When he saw that he was undone and his men slain, he was afraid that he himself would die. So he leaped aboard the ship. When he found this sword he drew it from its scabbard and went forth again. He found King Lambar and struck him on the helmet so heavily that he split both him and his horse. This was the first blow dealt by this sword in the kingdom of Logres. There resulted from it such a pestilence and persecution in the two kingdoms that never since had the land rendered its produce to the laborers. Since that time neither wheat nor any other crop has grown; trees have not borne fruit; nor have any fish been found in the waters. Therefore, the land of the two kingdoms had been called the "Terre Gaste" because it had been ruined by this fell stroke. [1] ✠

✠

Then, in my madness, I essayed
the door;
It gave; and thro' a stormy glare, a heat
As of a seventimes-heated furnace, I,
Blasted and burnt, and blinded as I was,
With such a fierceness that I
swooned away –
O, yet methought I saw the Holy Grail,
All palled in crimson samite, and around
Great angels, awful shapes, and
wings and eyes.'

ALFRED TENNYSON

The Holy Grail

In the midst of this joyful voyage comes a cloud of sorrow, which is transformed into a magnificent triumph of spirit over flesh. Perceval's sister, named Dindraine in some versions of the story, has followed the track of the Grail almost from the beginning, attaining a vision of the wondrous vessel before the Quest knights ever set forth. Now an even greater adventure awaits her – the passage into the realm of the spirit, which will affect not only her but also her companions.

Dindraine's role in the Grail story is a complex one. From the moment when, in her novices' cell, she sees a vision of the sacred vessel and the Quest, her own feet are set upon that way. Though not a knight, she follows her own road, which, in another text, she refers to as "a hard way." This is, indeed, the way of the mystic, demanding compete devotion to the task at hand and the kind of unshakable faith possessed by few. Yet, like many who undertake the Quest today, Dindraine has a sense of the outcome of the journey even before setting forth. She speaks to all those who stand upon the brink of the infinite and look into the depths. The shape of her soul-life is a perfect circle, its end already prefigured in its beginning. Her death is thus a triumph over life, and her passing merely takes her into the presence of the Grail and the infinite world to which it is merely a gateway. Her body, placed aboard a barge, is carried to the holy city of Sarras, the final resting place of the Grail. There, her spirit awaits the coming of her companions.

There is in this castle a gentlewoman to whom many years ago there fell a malady; and of no leech she could have remedy. But at the last an old man said if she might have a dish full of blood of a maid and a clean virgin in will and in work, and a king's daughter, that blood should be her health. "Now," said

Percivale's sister, "I see well that this gentlewoman is almost dead." "Indeed," said Galahad, "If ye bleed so much ye may die." "Truly," said she, "if I die to heal her I shall get me great worship and soul's health, and better is one harm than twain. And therefore there shall be no more battle, but to-morn I shall yield you your custom of this castle." And then there was great joy.

That night were the three fellows eased with the best; and on the morn they heard mass, and Sir Percivale's sister bade bring forth the sick lady. Then said she: "Who shall let my blood?" So one came forth and let her blood, and she bled so much that the dish was full. Then she lifted up her hand and blessed her; and then she said to the lady: "Madam, I am come to the death for to make you whole, for God's love pray for me." With that she fell in a swoon. Then Galahad and his two fellows lifted her up and staunched her, but she had bled so much that she might not live. Then she said when she was awaked: "Fair brother, Percivale, I die for the healing of this lady, so I require you that ye bury me not in this country, but as soon as I am dead put me in a boat at the next haven, and let me go as adventure will lead me; and then ye three come to the City of Sarras, there to achieve the Holy Grail, ye shall find me under a tower arrived, and there bury me in

the spiritual place; for there Galahad shall be buried, and ye also, in the same place."

Then Percivale understood these words, and granted it her, weeping. And then said a voice "Lords and fellows, tomorrow at the hour of prime ye three shall depart each from other, till the adventure bring you to the Maimed King." Then asked she her Saviour; and as soon as she had received it the soul departed from her body. And that same day was the lady healed. Then Sir Percivale made a letter of all that had happened to them, and put it in her right hand, and so laid her in a barge, and covered it with black silk; and so the wind arose, and drove the barge from the land, and all knights beheld it till it was out of their sight. Then they drew all to the castle, and so forthwith there fell a sudden tempest and a thunder, lightning, and rain, as all the earth would have broken. So half the castle turned up-so-down. So it passed evensong or the tempest was ceased. [2] ✠

From here the mystery grows deeper with each passing moment. The path of the Grail leads toward the final achievement of all adventures — and the start of another and even greater mystery. In the next passage, Galahad, Perceval, and Bors arrive at the Castle of the

Grail, where the answer to many questions and wonders is at last laid before them. The interpretation is once again highly mystical. The writers of this part of the tale were monks, and thus their personal vision of union with the divine takes the form of an appearance of Christ and a transfiguring celebration of the mass. In terms of our own Quest, the ultimate scene of attainment may take a very different form. The underlying message, however, is the same: to encounter the Grail, uncovered, directly, is to be in the presence of the infinite. The mystery here is that we may see nothing, but still be uplifted; that while our aspiration may be no more than a simple wish to live a better life, we may see the way to do so. This, as much as the great mystical events spoken of here, is part of the Grail also.

🕆 *And therewithal seemed to them that there came a man, and four angels from heaven, clothed in likeness of a bishop, with a cross in his hand; and these four angels bare him up in a chair, and set him down before the table of silver whereupon the Sangreal was; and it seemed that he had in midst of his forehead letters which said: "See ye here*

Joseph, the first bishop of Christendom, the same which Our Lord succoured in the city of Sarras in the spiritual place." Then the knights marvelled, for that bishop was dead more than three hundred year before. "O knights," said he, "marvel not, for I was sometime an earthly man." With that they heard the chamber door open, and there they saw angels; and two bare candles of wax, and the third a towel, and fourth a spear which bled marvellously, that three drops fell wihin a box which he held with his other hand. And they set the candles upon the table, and the third the towel upon the vessel, and the fourth the holy spear even upright upon the vessel. And then the bishop made as though he would have gone to the sacring of the mass. And at the lifting up there came a figure in likeness of a child, and his visage was as red and as bright as any fire, and smote himself into the bread, so that they all saw it that the bread was formed of a fleshly man; and then he put it into the Holy Vessel again. And then he went to Galahad and kissed him, and bade him go and kiss his fellows: and so he did anon. "Now," said he, "servants of Jesu Christ, ye shall be fed afore this table with sweet meats that never knights tasted." And when he had said, he vanished away. And they set them at the table in great dread, and made their prayers.

Then looked they and saw a man come out of the Holy Vessel, that had all the signs of the passion of Jesu Christ, bleeding all openly, and said: "My knights, and my servants, and my true children, which be come out of deadly life into spiritual life, I will now no longer hide me from you, but ye shall see now a part of my secrets and of my hidden things: now hold and receive the high meat which ye have so much desired." Then took he himself the Holy Vessel and came to Galahad; and he kneeled down, and there he received his Saviour, and after him so received all his fellows; and they thought it so sweet that it was marvellous to tell. Then said he to Galahad: "Son, wottest thou what I hold betwixt my hands?" "Nay," said he, "but if ye will tell me." "This is," said he, "the holy dish wherein I ate the lamb on Sheer-Thursday. And now hast thou seen that thou most desired to see, but yet hast thou not seen it so openly as thou shalt see it in the city of Sarras in the spiritual place. Therefore thou must go hence and bear with thee this Holy Vessel; for this night it shall depart from the realm of Logris, that it shall never be seen more here. And therefore go ye three to-morrow unto the sea, where ye shall find your ship ready, and no more with you but Sir Percivale and Sir Bors. Also I will that ye take with you of the blood of this spear for to anoint the Maimed

King, both his legs and all his body, and he shall have his health."

And Galahad went anon to the spear which lay upon the table, and touched the blood with his fingers, and came after to the Maimed King and anointed his legs. And therewith he started upon his feet out of his bed as an whole man, and thanked Our Lord that He had

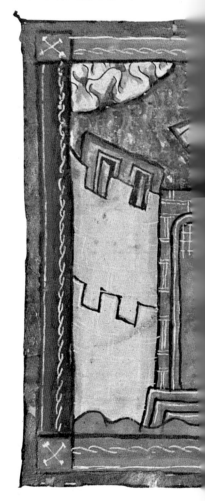

healed him. That same night about midnight came a voice among them which said: "My sons and not my chief sons, my friends and not my warriors, go ye hence where ye hope best to do and as I bade you." "Ah, thanked be Thou, Lord, that Thou wilt vouchsafe to call us, Thy sinners. Now may we well prove that we have not lost our pains."

And anon in all haste they took their harness and departed. ³ ✠

---------------------------- ✠ ----------------------------

THE STORY OF THE QUEST FOR THE HOLY GRAIL HAS INSPIRED GENERATIONS OF ARTISTS WHO HAVE ENSURED THAT IT REMAINS VIVIDLY ALIVE, FROM MONASTIC ILLUMINATED MANUSCRIPTS (BELOW) TO THE TAPESTRIES BY THE PRE-RAPHAELITE SIR EDWARD BURNE-JONES AND ALSO WILLIAM MORRIS (OVERLEAF).

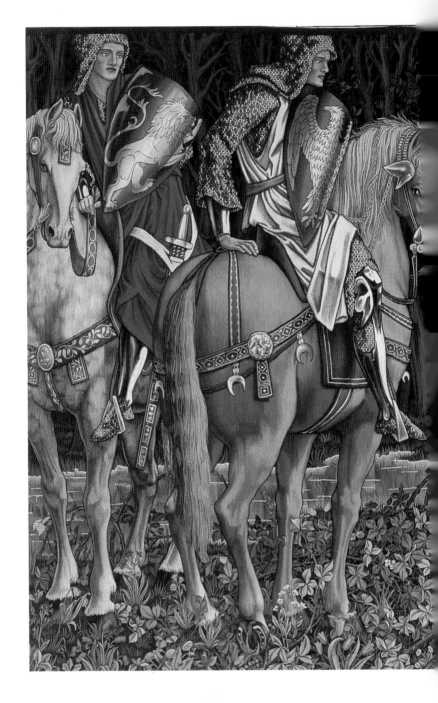

Thus is the Wounded King made whole, and the Waste Lands are made fruitful again. This simple metaphor tells us that in the midst of dryness, moisture can return. The wilderness of the Waste Land (whether it be in our own souls or in the outer world) is not forever. In the Grail story, the way is now open for the final acts of the Quest, the last miracles set forth in images of longing and attainment. With the events of the Achievement over, there is now only one road open to the initiates of the Grail – for such they now are – the way that leads beyond the confines of the outer world, into the realm of the spirit.

For Galahad, this means death of the flesh and passing to the realm of pure soul. For Perceval, it means the taking up of his own burden – the guardianship of that which he has sought for so long. For, when the Quest is finally ended, he must return to the Grail Castle and there await the coming of the next seeker, who may indeed be anyone who sets forth in search of personal truth, in pursuit of a path, or of adventure, or of the Grail itself. For the last of the Quest knights, Bors, it means a return to Camelot, to the realm of the

everyday, where he will tell of the events at the Grail Castle and beyond, and bear witness to the miracles of healing and restoration.

✠ *Right so departed Galahad, Percivale and Bors; and so they rode three days, and then they found the ship whereof the tale speaketh of to-fore. And when they came to the board they found in the midst the table of silver which they had left with the Maimed King, and the Sangreal which was covered with red samite. Then were they glad to have such things in the fellowship; and so they entered and made great reverence*

thereto; and Galahad fell in his prayer long time to Our Lord, that at what time he asked, that he should pass out of this world. So much he prayed till a voice said to him: "Galahad, thou shalt have thy request; and when thou askest the death of thy body thou shalt have it, and then shalt thou find the life of the soul." Percivale heard this, and prayed him, of fellowship that was between them, to tell him wherefore he asked such things. "That shall I tell you," said Galahad, "the other day when we saw a part of the adventures of the Sangreal I was in such a joy of heart, that I trow never man was that was earthly. And therefore I wot well, when my body is dead my soul shall be in great joy to see

the blessed Trinity every day, and the majesty of Our Lord, Jesu Christ."

So long were they in the ship that Galahad laid him down and slept a great while; and when he awaked he looked afore him and saw the city of Sarras. And as they would have landed they saw the ship wherein Percivale had put his sister in. "Truly," said Percivale, "in the name of God, well hath my sister held her covenant." Then took they out of the ship the table of silver, and he took it to Percivale and to Bors, to go tofore, and Galahad came behind. And right so they went to the city, and at the gate of the city they saw an old man crooked. Then Galahad called him and bade him help to bear this heavy thing.

"Truly," said the old man, "it is ten year ago that I might not go but with crutches." "Care thou not," said Galahad, "and arise up and shew thy good will." And so he assayed, and found himself as whole as ever he was. Then ran he to the table, and took one part against Galahad. And anon arose there great noise in the city, that a cripple was made whole by knights marvelous that entered into the gates of the city.

———————— ✠ ————————

ABOVE: THIS TAPESTRY BY SIR EDWARD BURNE-JONES SHOWS THE ATTAINMENT OF THE GRAIL BY THE THREE KNIGHTS: GALAHAD, THE PERFECT KNIGHT, WHO DIES IN BLISSFUL HAPPINESS; PERCEVAL WHO BECOMES THE GUARDIAN OF THE GRAIL; AND BORS WHO RETURNS TO THE COURT OF KING ARTHUR TO TELL THE WONDROUS TALES OF THE SACRED QUEST.

Then the three knights went to the water, and brought up into the palace Percivale's sister, and buried her as richly as a king's daughter ought to be. And when the king of the city, which was called Estorause, saw the fellowship, he asked them of whence they were, and what thing it was that they had brought upon the table of silver. And they told him the truth of the Sangreal, and the power which God had sent there. Then the king was a tyrant, and was come of the line of pagans, and took them and put them in prison in a deep hole.

But as soon as they were there Our Lord sent them the Sangreal, through whose grace they were always fulfilled while that they were in prison. So at the year's end it befell that this King of Estorause lay sick, and felt that he should die. Then he sent for the three knights, and they came afore him; and he cried them mercy for that he had done to them, and they forgave it him goodly; and he died anon. When the king was dead all the city was dismayed, and wist not who might be their king. Right so as they were in counsel there came a voice among them, and bade them choose the youngest knight of them three to be their king: "For he shall well maintain you and all yours." So they made Galahad king by all the assent of the holy city. And after he let make above the table of silver a chest of gold and of precious stones, that held the Holy Vessel. And every day early the three fellows would come afore it, and make their prayers to it.

Now at the year's end, after Galahad had borne the crown of gold, he arose up early along with his fellows, and came to the palace, and saw to-fore them the Holy Vessel, and a man kneeling on his knees in likeness of a bishop, that had about him a great fellowship of angels, as it had been Jesu Christ himself; and then he arose and began a mass of Our Lady. And when he came to the sacrament of the mass, and had done, anon he called Galahad, and said to him: "Come forth the servant of Jesu Christ, and thou shalt see that thou hast much desired to see." Then Galahad began to tremble right hard when the deadly flesh began to behold spiritual things. Then he held up his hands toward heaven and said: "Lord, I thank thee, for now I see that that hath been my desire many a day. Now, blessed Lord, would I not longer live, if it might please thee, Lord." And therewith the good man took Our Lord's body betwixt his hands, and proffered it to Galahad, and he received it right gladly and meekly. "Now wottest thou what I am?" said the good man. "Nay," said Galahad. "I am Joseph of Aramathie, the which Our Lord hath sent here to thee to bear thee fellowship; and know thou why he *hath sent me more than any other? For thou hast resembled me in two things; in that thou hast seen the marvels of the Sangreal, and in that thou hast been a clean maiden, as I have been and am."*

And when he had said these words Galahad went to Percivale and kissed him, and commended him to God; and so he went to Sir Bors and kissed him, and commended him to God, and said: "Fair lord, salute me to my lord, Sir Launcelot, my father, and as soon as ye see him, bid him remember of this unstable world." And therewith he kneeled down to-fore the table and made his prayers, and then suddenly his soul departed to Jesu Christ, and a great multitude of angels bare his soul up to heaven, that the two fellows might well behold it. Also the two fellows saw come from heaven an hand, but they saw not the body. And then it came right to the Vessel, and took it and the spear, and so bare it up to heaven. Since when was there never man so hardy to say that he has seen the Sangreal. ⁴

One book Dafydd has been told,
That he desires much more than gold;
The Book of the Blood,
of the Heroes' lays,
They that fell in Arthur's days:
The Book of Knights, the men renown'd
The Order of the Table Round:
The Book held in the Briton's hand,
That none can read in Horsa's land.
Dafydd of the Valle Crucis choir
Doth, Ifor, this fair book desire, –
This kingly book, which should he get
He would not crave for other meat.
A sound of friars is heard in Yale,
That cry too for the Holy Grail;
Nathless, it shall not tarry there
But back from Yale, let Gutto swear –
Your old blind Gutto! – soon shall be
Return'd, on his good surety.
So Heaven, out of St. David's guard,
Shall of its grace be thy reward.

A LETTER FROM THE POET
GUTTO TO IVOR TRAHAIARN
*Begging for the Book of the
Holy Grail (translated by
Ernest Rhys)*

But this is not quite yet the end of the story. For the Grail is, in some mysterious fashion, still present to us in our daily lives. The Quest may well be over for the age of Arthur — indeed, as was prophesied long ago, the kingdom of Logres would never be the same because of it. But the Grail remains an object of search, a mysterious goal that many more seekers will wish to attain. In this way, the Quest is seen to be only just beginning.

History tells us that Joseus stayed in a castle that had been King Fisherman's and shut himself in and lived upon whatever the Lord God might send him. He dwelled there long after Perceval had departed, and he died there. After his death, the dwelling began to fall into ruin, but the chapel remained as it always was, and is still so today. The place was far from people and seemed to be different. When it had fallen into decay, people wondered what was in the manor.

Various people went there but none dare enter it except two Welsh knights. They were handsome knights, young and light-hearted. Each promised the other to enter as an adventure. They remained within for a long time and when they came out they led the life of hermits and

wore hair shirts and lived in the forest and ate nothing but roots and led a hard life. Yet they seemed glad, and if they were asked why they rejoiced, they would say, "Go into the place where we have been and you shall know why." These two knights died without saying anything more, and they were called saints. ⁵

The Grail represents a truth that is close to the heart of Creation. As such, it draws us more deeply into that continuing process of becoming, where we experience the raw energy of life. Small wonder that all who set forth in search of the Grail are changed. It is the primary function of this marvelous vessel that it causes changes to occur in all who seek answers and are not afraid to ask questions. The process by which this takes place is as varied as the stars in the heavens and the number of souls upon the earth. No two people who set out on the Quest will be affected in the same way. The story of the Grail is one of the truly great "saving" stories, which can bring healing to all who read it with an open heart and mind. Yet it is paradoxical that it transcends the words that tell of it, the images that describe it, and the hearts that desire it. In the end, the Grail simply is, and no amount of words can make it other.

LEFT: SANC GRAEL BY DANTE GABRIEL ROSSETTI. GALAHAD, PERCEVAL, AND BORS RECEIVED SPIRITUAL NOURISHMENT WHEN THEY ACHIEVED THE HOLY GRAIL; BUT PERCEVAL'S SISTER FAILED TO ACHIEVE THE GRAIL BECAUSE SHE HAD SACRIFICED HER OWN LIFE TO HELP ANOTHER BEFORE THEIR QUEST WAS COMPLETE.

A–Z OF THE GRAIL

There are many aspects to the story of the Grail, some of which will be unfamiliar to those who have not encountered the Arthurian myths before. For the benefit of all such readers, there follows a list of the principal characters, places, and objects that are included in the book.

AMANGONS

King who is the supposed protector of the Maidens of the Wells. Desiring one of them, King Amangons rapes her and steals the golden cup with which she is wont to offer succor to weary travelers. When they see this, Amangon's men follow suit with others of the Maidens, thus causing an area of desolation that is known as the Waste Land.

ARTHUR, KING

Ruler of the semimythical realm of Logres and founder of the fellowship of the Round Table. His origins go back to the 6th century, when a warrior and leader of men named Artos, or Arthyr, led the feuding Celtic tribes of Britain to victory. Never forgotten, his character became enshrined in the memory of the people and grew in time into the legendary figure we know today.

BALIN LE SAUVAGE

A knight of Arthur's court who strikes the Dolorous Blow and causes the wounding of the Grail King Pellam. Balin first slays the evil Garlon, then, fleeing in fear, snatches up the sacred Grail spear and inflicts Pellam with a wound in the thigh. Balin subsequently dies in a patricidal conflict with his own brother.

BORS

Lancelot's cousin and the third of the successful Quest knights. He is, unlike his peers, a worldly man, whose simple determination to find the truth about the Grail carries him on to the end. He is the only one of the original fellowship to return with word of the events surrounding the Quest.

DINDRAINE

The sister of Perceval. She is brought up in a monastery and at an early age decides to follow the path of an anchoress, living a solitary life in a tiny cell in the forest. There she receives a vision of the Grail and sets forth on her own Quest. Later she joins Perceval and

Galahad. On arriving at a castle where a woman is sick with leprosy, she gives her blood to heal the woman and dies as a result. Her body is then placed in a magical ship and arrives at the sacred city of the Grail before any of her companions.

GALAHAD

Son of Lancelot and the Grail Princess. Brought up by monks and trained solely to go in Quest of the Grail, his early life is surrounded by signs and mysteries. His coming to Arthur's court proclaims the beginning of the Quest, and he is, above all, the most dedicated and pure of heart of all the knights.

GARLON

Brother to Pellam the Grail King, he is given to striking down his opponents while wearing a cloak of invisibility. He thus represents the shadow side of the Wounded King. He is slain by Balin, but his death is ultimately one of the causes of the Waste Land and the wounding of his brother.

GAWAIN

Cousin to King Arthur and one of the most renowned of the Round Table knights. He is the first to declare that he will search for the Grail but is only partially successful, due to his worldly nature. He nonetheless comes close to the heart of the mystery several times, and once releases a group of ghostly guardians who have remained in the service of the Grail beyond their allotted span on earth.

GRAIL

The sacred vessel sought by the knights of the Round Table. It provides healing and sustenance to those who come within its presence. In some texts it is associated with the Cauldron of Celtic tradition, in others with the Cup of the Last Supper.

GRAIL MAIDEN/PRINCESS.

Sometimes known as Elaine of Carbonek. She carries the Grail in the mysterious procession that passes through the hall of the Grail Castle to be witnessed by the hero. In later versions of the story she is the mother of Galahad, the successful Grail winner who supersedes Perceval.

GRAIL QUESTION

Usually written as "Whom does the Grail serve?", this is the all-important question, which, if asked by the Grail seeker, will set in motion the healing actions of the sacred vessel. In fact, it is often said that the asking of the question is more important than its answer, since the failure to act means to remain, like King Pelles, in a state of unhealing woundedness.

HERMIT

Brother to the Wounded King, Garlon, and to Perceval's mother, he is a saintly man whose part in the Grail Quest is to act as adviser, confessor, and guide to those who are seeking the miraculous vessel.

JOSEPH OF ARIMATHEA

Mentioned in biblical texts, he is known as the "uncle" of Christ. After the events of the Crucifixion he begged the body of Jesus from Pilate and had it buried in a tomb that was intended for his own use. Imprisoned as a follower of the new religion, he was visited by the risen Messiah in his cell and given the Grail. It sustained him until he was released many years later. Carrying the sacred relic, he subsequently set out on a long journey that was eventually to bring him to Britain.

LANCELOT

Perhaps the most famous of all the knights of the Round Table, he sought the Grail as an antidote to his illicit love for Arthur's queen. His son, Galahad, was to achieve the mysteries of the Grail more deeply than any of the other Quest knights who sought it.

LOGRES

The ancient name for King Arthur's Britain.

MAIDENS OF THE WELLS

Guardians of sacred wells scattered throughout the land of Logres. The Maidens serve all travelers who come their way, and speak with the Voices of the Wells, until King Amangons and his followers rape them and steal their golden cups. The result is the Waste Land, a sterile and wounded area around the Castle of the Grail.

MERLIN

King Arthur's counselor and adviser. The child of a mortal woman and an otherworldly being, he possessed the gifts of prophecy. He foresaw the coming of the Grail and attempted to prepare for it.

PERCEVAL

The archetypal hero of the Grail story. He grows up in isolation in the Waste Forest and is drawn to Arthur's court after meeting some knights. 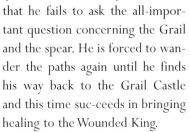 A simple and uncomplicated youth, he follows the advice of his mother and his knightly mentor so closely that he fails to ask the all-important question concerning the Grail and the spear. He is forced to wander the paths again until he finds his way back to the Grail Castle and this time suc-ceeds in bringing healing to the Wounded King.

ROUND TABLE

A fellowship of knights founded by Arthur and Merlin and dedicated to the upholding of law and order in the land of Logres. The knights took an oath to protect all those, especially women, who were in peril from evil-doers.

TITUREL

A wise and spiritual man who was vouchsafed a vision in later life to set up a temple to house the Grail. Aided by angelic hosts, he created one on top of Muntsalvach, the Mountain of Salvation.

WASTE LAND

An area of ruined and infertile land around the Grail Castle. Brought about as the result of the wounding 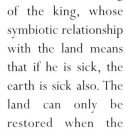 of the king, whose symbiotic relationship with the land means that if he is sick, the earth is sick also. The land can only be restored when the Wounded King is himself healed and the waters of life are allowed to flow again.

WOUNDED KING

Sometimes known by the name Pellam, at other times as Amfortas. The guardian of the Grail, who possesses an unhealing wound that can only be healed when the right person asks a ritual question concerning the mysterious Grail procession.

WIDOW OF THE WASTE FOREST

The mother of Perceval, who brings her son up in ignorance of knightly pursuits after her husband and older sons are killed in battle. She lives an utterly withdrawn life and dies soon after Perceval leaves her.

FURTHER READING

Of the many books which tell the story of the Grail in all its variety, here are just a few that will help those who wish to pursue their own quest more deeply.

TEXTS

CHRETIEN DE TROYES, *Perceval, or the Story of the Grail,* translated by Nigel Bryant. Cambridge: D.S. Brewer,1982

COMFORT, William W., *The Quest of the Holy Grail,* London: J.M.Dent,1926

EVANS, Sebastian, *The High History of the Holy Grail* [Perlesvaus], London: J.M.Dent, 1898

GUEST, Lady C., *The Mabinogion, Jones John,* Cardiff:1977

HEINRICH VON DEN TULIN, *The Crown,* translated by D.W.Thomas, Nebraska: University of Nebraska Press, 1989

LACY, N.J. et al.(eds), *The Lancelot-Grail: The Old French Arthurian Vulgate and Post-Vulgate in Translation* (5 Vols.), New York & London: Garland Publishing Inc., 1993–1995

LOOMIS, R.S. & L.H., *Medieval Romances,* New York: Random House,1957

MALORY, Sir Thomas, *Le Morte d'Arthur,* New York: University Books, 1961

MATARASSO, P., *The Quest of the Grail,* Harmondsworth: Penguin, 1969

MEEKS, J. & D., "The Temple of the Grail" [Albrecht von Scharfenburg] in *The Golden Blade,* London: Rudolf Steiner Press, 1981
ROBERT DE BORRON, *Joseph of Arimathea – A Romance of the Grail,* translated by Jean Rogers, London: Rudolf Steiner Press,1990

SKEELES, D., *The Romance of Perceval in Prose,* Seattle: University of Washington Press,1966

THOMPSON, A.W., *The Elucidation,* New York: Institute of French Studies, 1931

WESTON, J. L., *Parzival: A Knightly Epic,* London: Kegan Paul, Trench, Tubner, 1894

WESTON, J. L. *Sir Gawain at the Grail Castle,* London: D. Nutt, 1903

WILLIAMS, Robert Y., *Seint Greal,* 1876. Reprinted by Jones (Wales) Publishers, 1987

WOLFRAM VON ESCHENBACH, *Parzival,* translated by A. Hatto, Harmondsworth: Penguin, 1980

COMMENTARIES

ADOLF, H., *Visio Pacis: Holy City and Grail,* Pennsylvania State University Press, 1960

ASHE, G., *King Arthur's Avalon,* London: Fontana, 1973

BERGMANN, F. G., *The San Greal,* Edinburgh: Edmonston & Douglas, 1870

BOGDANOW, F., *The Romance of the Grail,* Manchester: Manchester University Press, 1966

BROWN, A. C. L., *The Origin of the Grail Legend,* Cambridge, Mass.: Harvard University Press, 1943

BRYCE, D., *The Mystical Way and the Arthurian Quest,* Llanerch, Dyfed: Llanerch Enterprises, 1986

CAVENDISH, R., *King Arthur and the Grail,* London: Weidenfeld & Nicolson, 1978

COUGHLAN, Ronan, *The Illustrated Encyclopedia of the Arthurian Legends,* Shaftsbury, Dorset: Element Books, 1993

CURRER-BRIGGS, N., *The Shroud and the Grail,* London: Weidenfeld & Nicolson, 1987

EVANS, S., *In Quest of the Holy Grail,* London: J. M. Dent, 1898

FORWARD, W. and Wolpert, A., *The Quest for the Grail* (The Golden Blade 47), Edinburgh: Floris Books, 1994

GILLIAM, R., Greenburg, M. H., and Kramer, E. E., (eds), *Grails: Quests, Visitations and Other Occurences,* Atlanta: Unnamable Press, 1992

HALL, M. P., *Orders of the Quest: The Holy Grail,* Los Angeles: The Philosophical Research Society, 1976

JOHNSON, K. and Elsbeth, M., *The Grail Castle: Male Myths and Mysteries in the Celtic Tradition,* St. Paul, MN: Llewellyn, 1995

JUNG, E, and Von Franz, M.-L., *The Grail Legends,* London: Hodder & Stoughton, 1971

KNIGHT, G., *The Secret Tradition in Arthurian Legend,* London: Aquarian Press, 1983

LACY, N. J. and Ashe, G., *The Arthurian Handbook,* New York: Garland Publishing Inc., 1986

LITTLETON, C. S. and Malcor, L. A., *From Scythia to Camelot: A Radical Reassessment of the Legends of King Arthur, the Knights of the Round Table, and the Holy Grail*, New York and London: Garland Press, 1994

LOOMIS, R.S., *The Grail From Celtic Myth to Christian Symbol*, Cardiff: University of Wales Press, 1963

MATTHEWS, C., *Arthur and the Sovereignty of Britain,* London: Arkana, 1989

MATTHEWS, C., *Elements of Celtic Tradition,* Shaftesbury, Dorset: Element Books, 1989

MATTHEWS, C., *Mabon and the Mysteries of Britain*, London: Arkana, 1987

MATTHEWS, J., *An Arthurian Reader,* London: Aquarian Press, 1988

MATTHEWS, J., *At the Table of the Grail,* London: Arkana, 1987

MATTHEWS, J., *Elements of Arthurian Tradition,* Shaftesbury, Dorset: Element Books, 1989

MATTHEWS, J., *The Grail, Quest for Eternal Life,* London: Thames & Hudson, 1981

MATTHEWS, J., *A Glastonbury Reader,* London: Aquarian Press, 1991

MATHEWS, J., *Healing The Wounded King*, Shaftsbury, Dorset: Element Books, 1997

MATTHEWS, J., *The Household of the Grail,* London: Aquarian Press, 1990

MATTHEWS, J., *King Arthur and the Grail Quest,* London: Cassell, 1994

MATTHEWS, J., *Sources of the Grail,* Edinburgh: Floris Books, 1996

MATTHEWS, J., *Within the Hollow Hills,* Edinburgh: Floris Books, 1994

MATTHEWS, J. & C., *The Arthurian Book of Days,* London: Sidgwick & Jackson/New York: St Martins, 1990

MATTHEWS, J. & C., *The Arthurian Tarot: A Hallowquest,* London: Aquarian Press, 1990

MATTHEWS, J.& C., *Ladies of the Lake,* London: Aquarian Press, 1992

MATTHEWS, J. and Green, M., *The Grail Seekers Companion,* London: Aquarian Press, 1988

MORDUCH, A., *The Sovereign Adventure,* Edinburgh: James Clarke, 1970

NUTT, A., *Studies on the Legend of the Holy Grail,* New York: Cooper Square Publishers, 1965

OLSCHEKI, L., *The Grail Castle and its Mysteries,* Manchester: Manchester University Press, 1966

ROLT-WHEELER, F., *Mystic Gleams from the Holy Grail,* London: Rider, [c.1945]

SCHLAUCH, Margaret, *Medieval Narrative: A Book of Translations,* New York: Geordian Press, 1969

STEIN, Walter Johannes, T*he Ninth Century: World History in the Light of the Holy Grail,* (with an introduction by John Matthews), London: Temple Lodge Press, 1991

SUSSMAN, L., *The Speech of the Grail,* New Hampshire: Lindisfarne Press, 1995

WESTON, J. L., *From Ritual to Romance,* New York: Doubleday, 1957

WESTON, J. L., *The Quest of the Holy Grail,* London: G. Bell & Sons, 1913

WILLIAMS, C., *Arthurian Poets Williams,* edited by D.L. Dodds, Woodbridge: The Boydell Press, 1994 [includes *Taliessin through Logres* and *The Region of the Summer Stars*]

COURSES

John and Caitlin Matthews offer courses on the Grail, Shamanism, and Celtic Traditions. For further information on these, upcoming publications, and other events, send 6 first-class stamps (U.K.) or 6 International Reply Paid Coupons (elsewhere) for a sample copy of The Hallowquest Newsletter, to: BCM Hallowquest, London WC1N 3XX.

NOTES

Chapter One
THE COMING OF THE GRAIL

1. Adapted from *The History of the Holy Grail* by Robert De Borron, translated by Margaret Schlauch, Allen & Unwin, 1928

2. Adapted from *The Younger Titurel* by Albrecht Von Scharfenberg, translated by J. & D. Meeks, *The Golden Blade*, 1981

3. Adapted from *Le Morte d'Arthur,* Book II, chs. 14 & 15, by Sir Thomas Malory, New York University Books, 1964

4. Adapted from *Perlesvaus* by anon., translated by S. Evans, Temple Classics, 1898

5. Adapted from *Le Morte d'Arthur,* Book XI, chs. 1 & 2, by Sir Thomas Malory

Chapter Two
THE QUEST BEGINS

1. Adapted from *Le Morte d'Arthur,* Book XIV, ch. 2, by Sir Thomas Malory

2. Adapted from *Perceval, or the Story of the Grail* by Chrétien de Troyes, translated by R.S. and L.H. Loomis, Random House, 1947

3. Adapted from *Le Morte d'Arthur,* Book XIII, ch.1, by Sir Thomas Malory

4. Adapted from *Le Morte d'Arthur,* Book XIII, ch.2, by Sir Thomas Malory

5. Adapted from *Perlesvaus* by anon., translated by S. Evans

6. Adapted from *Le Morte d'Arthur,* Book XIII, ch.4, by Sir Thomas Malory

Chapter Three
LANDS OF WASTE AND WONDER

1. Adapted from *Perceval, or the Story of the Grail* by Chrétien de Troyes, translated by R.S. and L.H. Loomis

2. Adapted from *The Elucidation* by anon., translated by S. Evans, J.M. Dent, 1898

3. Adapted from *The Quest for the Holy Grail* by anon., translated by W.W. Comfort, J.M. Dent, 1926

4. Adapted from *The Prose Lancelot,* by anon., translated by J.L. Weston, J.M. Dent, 1903

5. Adapted from *Le Morte d'Arthur,* Book XVI, ch.9, by Sir Thomas Malory

Chapter Four
THE QUEST DEEPENS

1. Adapted from *Perlesvaus* by anon., translated by S. Evans

2. Adapted from *Le Morte d'Arthur,* Book XV, chs. 3 & 4, by Sir Thomas Malory

3. Adapted from *Parzifal: A Knightly Epic* by Wilfram von Eschenbach, translated by J.L. Weston, London, 1894

4. Adapted from *The Crown* by Heinrich Von Deus Turlin, translated by J.L Weston, J.M. Dent, 1903

Chapter Five
ACHIEVEMENT

1. Adapted from *The Quest for the Holy Grail* by anon., translated by W.W. Comfort

2. Adapted from *Le Morte d'Arthur,* Book XVII, ch.2, by Sir Thomas Malory

3. Adapted from *Le Morte d'Arthur,* Book XVII, chs. 20 & 21, by Sir Thomas Malory

4. Adapted from *Le Morte d'Arthur,* Book XVII, chs. 21 & 22, by Sir Thomas Malory

5. Adapted from *Perlevaus* by anon., translated by S. Evans

INDEX